HORSE SENSE FROM THE HEARTLAND

DANIEL C. BRUCH

CONTENTS

Preface vii
Introduction ix

SECTION I
Common Sense Thinking about the Family

1. The Human Family 3
2. My Tribe 5
3. E Pluribus Unum: My Extended Family 7
4. My Biological Family: Genomes, Evolution, and Diversity 10
5. In Her Own Words 13
6. Looking at My Family: Our Mirror Images 15
7. A Radical (Meaning "Root Cause") View of Mother's Day 18
8. April Fools' Day Thoughts 21
9. Good Trouble? 23
10. International Women's Day Is for Men 25
11. Conflicted Beginnings – Hopeful Expectations 27

SECTION II
Common Sense Thinking about the Government

12. Proposing a Purple Reign 31
13. A Test of Character 34
14. Why Are We Interested in Civil Behavior? 36
15. Thoughts About Presidents' Day 38
16. Thinking about Patriotism 40
17. Government and Guns 42
18. The Eleventh Hour of the Eleventh Day of the Eleventh Month 44
19. Peace Officers? Rethinking a Name 46
20. Rescind the Second Amendment 48
21. Blessed Are the Restless 50
22. Low Turnout Equals Poor Government 53
23. The Duty of Youth 55
24. Gridlock About Memorial Day? 58

25. Grace and Mercy   60
26. An Apothegm of Historical Import   62
27. About January 6: "…casting about to preserve their reputations…"   65
28. An Irate, Tireless Minority…   67
29. Government for the Few, Paid for by the Many   70
30. A Reformation Thought before Any Election   73

SECTION III
Common Sense Thinking about Religion

31. A Common Base   77
32. Resetting Our Moral Compass   79
33. A Divine Idea   81
34. Majoring in Minors?   84
35. Separation of Church and State   86
36. Halloween: Religious and Secular   89
37. Thanksgiving a Myth?   91
38. Just Wondering?   94
39. "We're Here for Something Else besides Ourselves."   97
40. A Hopeful Christmas Wish   100
41. Thoughts About Flag Waving on Entering a New Year   102
42. In This New Year, I Still Find It Difficult To Admit Being a Christian   105
43. An Epiphany Wish: Reason and Reasonableness   108
44. Blessed are the Flexible…   110
45. Patriotism: Wholesome or Harmful?   112
46. Compassion toward Others   115

SECTION IV
Common Sense Thinking about Education

47. No One Has a Monopoly on Truth or Wisdom   119
48. As Our School Year Comes to a Close…   122
49. Horace Who?   124
50. National Teacher's Day   127
51. "My Dear Children"   129
52. A School Teacher, the State of Wisconsin, and National Flag Day!   131
53. It Should End There   134
54. "Anger Is an Acid …."   136
55. Earth Month: Our Planet, Our State, Our City   139

SECTION V
Common Sense Thinking About the Economy

56. Why Is It So Scary?   143
57. "Stuck on Stupid"   145
58. It Depends on What You Call It!   147
59. Afraid of the Light   149
60. Being an Entrepreneur   152
61. How Could It Be Worse?   154
62. Honesty and Wisdom   156
63. Watching What People Do   159
64. George Orwell, Again   161
65. Promoting Human Welfare   163
66. Grafters and Grifters   165
67. How Long Will it Take?   167

About the Author   171

PREFACE

I am a heartlander, born in Iowa USA in 1939. Most of my formative youth was spent in Iowa. My educational journey expanded my personal heartland to include the states of Minnesota, Wisconsin, Illinois, and Indiana. It was primarily in those locales that my values were learned, and civic virtues were practiced. Many of those values and virtues have been challenged by change. An increased emphasis on individualism, a growing distrust of government, an expansion of tribalism and distrust of others, and a growing fear of the future are some of the contributing factors.

Over a decade ago, I began writing columns for a local hometown Wisconsin newspaper, the *Hudson Star Observer*, as a means of providing reasoned and reasonable (in my opinion!) responses to those changes. Many of those edited articles are included here in response to readers who have asked for such a compilation. Small-town newspapers continue to struggle for existence, and I thank the five editors and five owners who have valiantly continued the journey to provide a forum for writers like me.

Not everyone in my family shares my enthusiasm for Iowa, but all have been my staunchest and skilled editors and critics with a combination of intellect and caution that has mostly kept me centered. The fact that my spouse and daughters have four doctorates, four master's degrees, and one law degree among them adds credibility to their critiques. For them I remain deeply grateful.

It was Will Rogers, an American humorist and Oklahoma-born heartlander, who said that "common sense ain't common." I expect that what lies ahead in your reading will add credence to that comment. The contents share the common-sense values and virtues learned in my youth, and still predominate in the world in which I have lived. In spite of all the public screaming and shouting and despicable behavior of many in public and private life, who pretend to convey common sense, the majority of us live our lives in a quieter confidence, demonstrating common-sense "horse sense" in a very expansive heartland.

INTRODUCTION

Horse sense? When presenting a series of thoughts and ideas that seek to provide reasonable understanding, using a horse as an indicator of enlightenment seems far-fetched. Why not "wise as an owl" or "smart as a fox" as alternative animals of choice? Having been born and raised in pre-1950 Iowa, I grew up with expressions that referred to horses. Plants that looked like another but were bigger and gristlier were called "horse-something." Horseradish (resembles a radish but with a much stronger taste) is an example. Horsefly, or horselaugh, are also common expressions.

In the same manner, I also learned to use the word *horse* as a prefix to define something as unlikely or comic, like in horsefeathers or horseplay or horsefiddle.

Using the word *horse* as a prefix in Iowa simply acknowledged that horses held an important place in the lives of the people. It also, in a review of etymological history, harkens back to medieval England where present-day English was largely formed. In both cases, the adding of *horse* to *sense* was meant to convey an unsophisticated, country type of sense that assumed an intellectual ability of those who exceed others in practical wisdom. The type of sense that was a common-sense alternative to the armchair, but inexperienced, opinionating of those who expressed knowledge that seemed to be untouched by common sense. W. C. Fields is credited with expressing this understanding from a horse's point of view when he said, "Horse sense is the thing a horse has which keeps it from betting on people."

The term *heartland* refers to "the central geographical region of the US in which mainstream or traditional values predominate," according to the Merriam-Webster dictionary. Limiting our thoughts for the moment to the Midwestern United States, those values as I remember them were the ones taught and instilled in us as children. They included the family values of respect for others, love, honor, loyalty, self-discipline, and respect for God and country. In other words, we were expected to lead principled and value-centered lives, with what the early philosophers called civic virtues.

It is good to note here that the definition of the heartland has changed over the years. Among some, the current thinking defines the "new" heartland as encompassing all the central United States, from the Canadian border to the southern coast, leaving out the East and West Coast states. It must also be acknowledged that a desire to lead principled and value-centered lives can be claimed by many in the United States without regard to geographical location, and throughout the world as well.

The principles and values that earlier were defined as "unsophisticated, common-sense, practical wisdom" shared by a significant group of people, are defined by sociologists as social norms that prevail in our social institutions. In other words, ways we are expected to behave and things we are expected to believe that are centered around our shared human needs. These are called the primary human institutions, namely: family, government, education, the economy, and religion.

What follows are some "unsophisticated, common-sense" perspectives about principles and values related to our commonly held social norms.

A NOTE ABOUT NAME-CALLING

We are living in a time when our country has been divided into the reds and the blues, the conservatives, and the liberals. It is the assumption throughout these pages that conservatives and liberals each have their role to play. When one considers all the etymological history of these two words, conservatives seem best defined as those who are generally predisposed to resist change. Liberals, for the same reason, are defined as generally predisposed to encourage and support change.

Cross-culturally, humans seem to be predominantly resistant to change and most comfortable with the status quo. Conservatives are, therefore, not an endangered species and not likely to become one. Being comfortable with the status quo is not a negative attribute. Sociologists tell us that the social organization that is a part of maintaining the status quo is necessary for an orderly society. Without a majority of people wanting to stay where they are and do what they are doing, the consequent social change would likely lead to more social disorganization than a society could long endure. We need conservatives and appreciate the social stability they bring to our culture.

We also need liberals. They serve as a cultural balance to challenge and to inspire those who are comfortable with things as they are. Liberals almost always constitute a minority because their disposition toward change can confound the majority, frighten some, worry more, and often challenge predominant social assumptions. It might be easier not to have them around, but without the balance and impetus toward change that they bring, social life would stagnate.

We need each other. Most people have elements of traditional conservatism and liberalism woven within their personal and world views. Most people with whom we speak and with whom we have regular contact are neither totally "red" nor totally "blue" in the sense of current political and divisive jargon. Rather, we are a combination of both colors blending into varying shades of purple. We also share some common values that speak to us about the conflicted issues of the day. What we have not been very good at is simply speaking to one another to find those common values and civic virtues that can draw us together. The following pages are intended to reflect the common values and civic virtues that, to one degree or another, we all share.

SECTION I

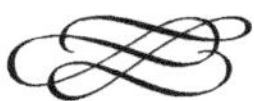

COMMON SENSE THINKING ABOUT THE FAMILY

fam·i·ly ˈfam-lē : the basic unit in society traditionally consisting of two parents rearing their children *also* : any of various social units differing from but regarded as equivalent to the traditional family

THE HUMAN FAMILY

Almost eighty years ago, Mahatma Gandhi said that "the world has enough for everyone's need, but not everyone's greed." He was concerned about our human greed that was consuming the planet's resources as the world population was rapidly growing. Over fifty years ago, the Zero Population Growth organization, begun by Paul Ehrlich, a Stanford University professor, argued that it was time for a population-control movement. Ehrlich believed that the world would face shortages of water, food, and more if population growth was not reduced.

Because population growth of the world has increased steadily since the Medieval times, people remain interested in its progress. It was on July 11, 1987, that the world's population reached five billion people, and it was called "Five Billion Day." This prompted the United Nations Population Fund to create World Population Day, now celebrated annually on July 11. Since then, according to the UN Population Fund, there were an estimated 7 billion people on October 31, 2011. As for current numbers (2023), the World Population Clock now shows there are over 333 million people in the United States, and eight billion people worldwide.

Shortly after the formation of the Zero Population Growth movement in 1968, it became obvious that the topic of world population had been one of immediate concern for at least twenty-five centuries. For example, the philosopher Confucius (551–479 BC) said, "Excessive [population] growth may reduce output per worker, repress levels of living for the masses and engender strife." Aristotle (384–322 BC) said, "One would have thought that it was even more necessary to limit population than property. The neglect of this subject, which in existing states is so common, is a never-failing cause of poverty among the citizens; and poverty is the parent of both revolution and crime." Tertullian, a writer, and theologian (AD 160–220) said that "the strongest witness is the vast population of the Earth to which we are a burden, and she scarcely can provide for our needs."

One can see that the concern about too much population growth on our planet has been with us from far in our past and continues until this day. In short, the question remains: how many people will our planet hold? The shortest and best answer is, "We don't know." Each year, according to current estimates, roughly 83 million people are added to the world's population. Considering that fertility levels are expected to continue to decline, our planet's population is expected nonetheless to reach 8.6 billion in 2030, 9.8 billion in 2050, and 11.2 billion in 2100.

Because of the millions of people now added to our planet's population annually, the United Nations seeks to promote awareness of the many related social issues, especially the importance of family planning, gender equality, poverty, maternal health, and human rights. In 2023, World Population Day was focused on "a world of 8 billion: towards a resilient future for all—harnessing opportunities and ensuring rights and choices for all."

All these issues may be best addressed by remembering Gandhi's encouragement to prioritize need rather than greed in each of our lives.

MY TRIBE

In so many respects, the past few years have been tumultuous years. Politically, we had two presidential impeachments. We also saw the same person, Donald J. Trump, indicted on both state and federal criminal charges. Scientifically, we inched closer to the tipping point of climate change. Financially, our economic inequality kept growing. Socially, we continued to separate ourselves from one another. Religiously, we continued to be less interested in matters of religious faith and more exclusive in terms of those with whom we choose to worship. In family matters, the US now has the world's highest rate of children living in single-parent homes. Educationally, teacher pay continues to fall and educational disparity between states continues to grow. So likely this is a good time to reflect upon and reposition our thinking about **truthfulness, tribalism, and turmoil**—all aspects of the realities expressed above.

Regarding **truthfulness**, this time in history has been called the post-truth era. *Post-truth* (Oxford Dictionary's 2016 word of the year) is used to identify those who believe that objective facts are less important than feelings and personal beliefs in determining behaviors. In other words, two kinds of "truth" now prevail. Truth, as ordinarily defined, is any proposition based upon objective facts, devoid of bias influenced by human feelings. Speaking the truth refers to one's ability to judge a fact or proposition without being partial or influenced by personal factors. Traditional truth is based upon objective reasoning and empirical evidence, while post-truth is based upon human-fabricated notions that gain wide acceptance as truth. Post-truths are often engineered to benefit a self-interest rather than benefit the good of society.

Then there is **tribalism**. The word *tribe* is an English word dating from the 13th century and likely derived from the Latin word *tres*. *Tres* refers to the three tribes into which the Roman people were originally divided. In current thought, we usually define tribalism as the loyalties we have toward particular groups and how those loyalties affect our behavior and attitudes toward others. Each of us is vulnerable to believing that the ideas we have are well-reasoned and principled. Often, however, they are adopted from and defended as a part of the tribe(s) to which we belong. We all find meaning when we belong to an ideological, religious, political, or cultural tribe. Because of that, it takes significant personal honesty and strength to examine our own ideas as scrupulously as we do other people's ideas, to really listen to other arguments, and to be open to discarding our own bad ideas. It is really the only way to begin the tentative and difficult move into an unfamiliar mental landscape of discovery and knowledge.

Finally, there is **turmoil**. It is defined as "a state or condition of extreme confusion, agitation, or commotion." It may be that in 2023, the use of the word "turmoil" is a bit stark. These are, however, times of great uncertainty. It is in these times that trying harder to live up to the following two resolutions could provide hope for change: 1) I will work harder to discern the objective truth about facts and propositions; and 2) I will work harder to examine my own ideas and beliefs for their objective validity apart from tribal definitions. Truth becomes our moral compass in times of uncertainty and turmoil, and where there is a strong societal belief in the priority of truthfulness and openness to others, reasonableness and humility will thrive.

E PLURIBUS UNUM: MY EXTENDED FAMILY

There is much concern about the rise of domestically led terrorism and violence these past five years. Essentially without exception, it has been directed against people of color, particularly African Americans, Hispanics, and Asians. It is interesting that apart from the indigenous Native Americans, historical realities remind us that African Americans have been within our shores since 1492, Hispanics since 1533, and Asians since 1587. During 2020, for the first time in our history, non-white people and Hispanics made up the predominant number of those who are age sixteen and younger and living in the US. A non-white majority US population is now predicted within the next two decades. Given those realities, one can see why the original national motto of the United States is again being mentioned in public discourse.

E Pluribus Unum is a phrase that was used in a poem attributed to Virgil, by St. Augustine in Book IV of the *Confessions, by* Cicero in his *De Officiis,* and also by several others. Even the Wizard in *The Wizard of Oz* gives the scarecrow a diploma from "The Society of E Pluribus Unum." The phrase is most accurately defined as "out of many, one." Given the rich history of the phrase, it is only appropriate that the founders of the United States of America chose this to be our original motto. It was adopted by an Act of Congress in 1782 and has been used on paper money and coins since 1795.

"Out of many, one." We have had a known diversity of peoples on our continent since the thirteenth century. Eight centuries later, we count our ancestors as having come from virtually every country and part of the world. Our backgrounds are many, yet the values to which we subscribe in our Constitution and other founding documents are one and the same for all of us. Our stated fundamental beliefs endorse our shared innate license to expect life, liberty, the pursuit of happiness, the common good, justice, equality, diversity, truth, sovereignty, and patriotism. The Constitutional principles that serve as the foundation for our beliefs are the rule of law, the separation of powers, representative government, checks and balances, individual rights, freedom of religion, federalism, and the civilian control of our military.

Since the birth of our nation, we have lived under a dual system in the application of Constitutional principles — one for white people and another for people of color. In the past few years, domestic terrorism and white nationalism have become a far greater threat than any other type of terrorism. Recent research suggests that the one thing domestic white terrorists likely have in common is that they are deeply afraid of loss — loss of the way life used to be (real or imagined) and the way they want it to be. They see their future threatened by people of color and those who support them and fear the loss of their perceived importance in society.

But whatever the reason, they become, to varying degrees, less affected by the restraints of guilt, compassion, and empathy, and may feel personally justified in their harmful actions. We who desire to work toward a more perfect, inclusive Union find it again to be a time to stand together to help create necessary legal changes. This starts with voting. It is increasingly obvious that some of those we have hired to represent us have been failing us and have become antagonistic to the government to which they pledged their support and that pays their salaries. Consider voting them out of office. "Out of many, one." It is up to us. Consider again making decisions based on what we have always aspired to be as a nation, rather than on real or supposed past heartbreaks or infringements and move toward the light of a brighter future. We can do this with a new, shared will that binds us together, because we really are one, out of many.

MY BIOLOGICAL FAMILY: GENOMES, EVOLUTION, AND DIVERSITY

A few years after the National Geographic Society initiated their Genographic Project, many people sent in their DNA samples and found out their genetic ancestry. What a surprise it was for all to see that our ancestors had wandered from Africa throughout most of the other continents of our world. We are all the very definition of mongrelization. Our ancestors picked up a bit of genetic material here, more there, a touch there, etc.

Our genomes (all genetic material of an organism) and their journey through history also provide the perfect definition of evolution. Merriam-Webster defines evolution as "the historical development of a biological group (such as a species)," which in our case is *Homo sapiens*. The point of this all is that our genomic mixing and blending over the millennia, the evolutionary journey, is the essence of diversity. And diversity is once again a part of the public conversation in many communities, most of which are predominantly white. Already, objections to the process have also arisen in many areas.

The objections are difficult to understand. From the most ancient of times, there is compelling evidence that various races of the world traded and interacted with each other. Diversity has been one of the leading survival tactics of humans. It opens the mind and breaks down barriers. It is the very essence of nature with the diversity of colors, the variations of seasons, the movements of sun, moon, and stars in harmony and in coordination. We humans are small constituents of this vast cosmic space, making it imperative to respect and greet the great human variation present around us. People hailing from different cultures, ethnicities, races, countries, or religions are just parts of the one human family.

If we were to limit our discussion to science, the variations among humans are easy to explain. The basis for skin color depends, in part, upon geographical and environmental factors. In addition, it is the pigment melanin that determines the precise shade of skin. So, the main point is that nowhere in the description of humans lies any factor that makes a particular race better than others. The genetics of a human body are at least 99.99% the very same all over the world. Discrimination, therefore, on any basis is both unjustified and unacceptable.

Why should communities embrace increased diversity? Because our international boundaries are continuing to shrink. Because trade among the countries continues to increase. Because no country, including our own, can survive on its own. Because collaboration and cooperation among all parts of the world are mandatory for our survival. We all depend on diverse peoples for a better market and an energetic workforce. So why not accept an increasingly diverse population gracefully, because it will help in building a more congenial environment in a wonderful place to live?

It has always been the responsibility of older generations to understand and teach their younger ones the importance and acceptance of diverse peoples among and around us. We know from experience that warmly embracing the diverse cultures and religions and their teachings helps to improve the human race as a whole and will lead toward a better future for generations to follow. Because, as President Jimmy Carter said, "We have become not a melting pot but a beautiful mosaic. Different people, different beliefs, different yearnings, different hopes, different dreams." But one human race. Regarding our human race, "We hold these truths to be self-evident, that all men are created equal."

IN HER OWN WORDS

Pride Month has just ended. Depending upon the poll being used, about 80% of Americans support LGBTQ+ perspectives and activities. According to the US Census Bureau Household Pulse Survey, only about 8% of our population identifies as GLBTQ+ with only 0.6% of those identifying as Transexual. Based upon the information provided by world surveys, the most recent findings show about 3% of respondents declared themselves to be homosexual, gay, or lesbian, while 4% identify as bisexual. Additionally, 1% are pansexual or omnisexual.

What has always interested me is that in the broader animal world, the same basic proportions prevail. Same sex behavior among animals has been documented in wildlife since the 1700's, even though scientific study of such behaviors is relatively more recent. Currently, about 1500 different species of wildlife are known to practice same sex behaviors. The species come from all the major groups of animals including birds, reptiles, fish, arthropods, mollusks and, of course, all the mammals—including humans.

Given that a portion of all species practice same sex activities, it seems to be within the normal ordering of the animal world. Some portion of the animal world swims, some portion flies, some portion walks upright, some portion has red hair (1 to 2%), and some portion exhibits same sex preferences. Thanks for the differences! Diversity is a gift that takes the boredom out of uniformity! So why do some of us have a difficult time accepting the normalcy of such diverse sexual behavior? It occurs within a statistical minority, but that does not make it abnormal behavior for some.

Years ago in my teaching I used a series entitled "In Their Own Words." It had letters written by slaves to provide an understanding about the actual experiences and feelings of slaves in the US. I asked a long-term friend of mine who is a member of the LGBTQ+ community to do the same.

Here is part of what she shared:

"My gender identity and sexual orientation are only a small part of who I am. I am a daughter, sister, and aunt. I am a single, white, Norden, Christian female who is a professional ethics review board member and caregiver to aging parents. Other identities I carry include naturalist, kayaker, gardener, world traveler, mystery book reader, movie goer, wine consumer, and a Disney addict. But because of being "different" in one aspect of my life, people who I thought were good friends, have abandoned me (what might be called "cancel culture" today) and I have listened to harsh judgment from the pulpit of my church (forcing me to find a more inclusive church community). These rejections and judgments make this one small part of who I am loom large and, unfortunately, not in a positive life-enhancing way. For me, it has more to do with companionship. A relationship of give and take, mutual understanding, compassion, and forgiveness. It is about being in relationship with a person with whom I would like to share life's joys, sorrows, and trials with just like anyone else." Well, that sounds normal to me.

LOOKING AT MY FAMILY: OUR MIRROR IMAGES

I t was Goethe who said that "behavior is the mirror in which everyone shows their image." Our shared cultural and country images have become clouded in the last decades and, more recently, shattered. Our "happiness" rating (USA) has dropped to sixteenth in the world; we have stagnating or declining real wages, a rapidly expanding gap between rich and poor, overproduction of young graduates with advanced degrees, and exploding public debt.

What has happened to us? Less than fifteen years ago, the first African American was elected President of our country, and many of us seemed thrilled about beginning a new era of racial, cultural, and economic equality and peace. Instead, as 2023 stumbles uncertainly onward, the ugly head of racism continues to show itself, our culture is increasingly divided, and nationalism and white supremacy seem to keep growing. According to the Southern Poverty Law Center, there are now 940 hate groups currently operating in the USA, with 15 hate groups in Wisconsin, 12 in Minnesota, and 3 in Iowa.

Our past President was disapproved by 60 percent of our population, our current President has nearly matched that number of disapproval, 83 percent disapprove of our Congress, every day over 100 people are killed by a gun with twice as many injured by guns each day, and 75 percent of our population thinks our country is heading in the wrong direction. The sainted Maya Angelou reminds us of where such negativity leads us when she said, "Hate, it has caused a lot of problems in the world but has not solved one yet." As Jesus, quoted by Abraham Lincoln, said, "A house divided against itself cannot stand."

So how can we begin again to turn things around? How about listening to some folks who always seemed to appeal to our better selves? For example:

"An individual has not started living until he can rise above the narrow confines of his individualistic concerns to the broader concerns of all humanity." — Martin Luther King, Jr.

"Ultimately, America's answer to the intolerant man is diversity." — Robert Kennedy

"It is time for parents to teach young people early on that in diversity there is beauty and there is strength." — Maya Angelou

"We need to help students and parents cherish and preserve the ethnic and cultural diversity that nourishes and strengthens this community—and this nation." — Cesar Chavez

"We need to give each other the space to grow, to be ourselves, to exercise our diversity. We need to give each other space so that we may both give and receive such beautiful things as ideas, openness, dignity, joy, healing, and inclusion." — Max de Pree

"Diversity: the art of thinking independently together." — Malcolm Forbes

"Diversity in the world is a basic characteristic of human society, and also the key condition for a lively and dynamic world as we see today." — Jintao Hu

"A lot of different flowers make a bouquet." — Muslim Origin

"Isn't it amazing that we are all made in God's image, and yet there is so much diversity among his people?" — Desmond Tutu

Read, reflect, revise, renew, and re-energize for seeking the common good. What we now need is a new social contract that will empower us to move beyond extreme polarization and find consensus. Toward that end, we will have to again tip the shares of economic growth and justice back toward workers while also improving government funding for public health, education, and infrastructure. May our behavior reflect the image of a nation seeking "liberty [freedom] and justice for all." Because, yes, "Behavior is the mirror in which everyone shows their image."

A RADICAL (MEANING "ROOT CAUSE") VIEW OF MOTHER'S DAY

It was the American novelist, Barbara Kingsolver, who said that "kids don't stay with you if you do it right. It's the one job where, the better you are, the more surely you won't be needed in the long run." There are moments when, as a parent, this becomes a difficult reality with which to live. We raise our children to become independent and, most often, they do! Then, while rejoicing about that fact, come the sadness and void concomitant with loss. Generation after generation, the cycle repeats as does the love of mothers who, in large part, make it happen. So when did we begin to publicly recognize the importance of mothers?

In the United States, we began to recognize the essential and difficult work of mothering in 1876 when Anna Jarvis, an Appalachian homemaker, organized a day to raise awareness of poor health conditions in her community, a cause she believed would be best advocated by mothers. She called it "Mother's Work Day." Then in 1901, Julia Ward Howe, a Boston poet, pacifist, suffragist, and author of the lyrics to the "Battle Hymn of the Republic," organized a day encouraging mothers to rally for peace, since she believed mothers mourned the loss of human life more harshly than anyone else.

When Anna Jarvis died, her daughter, also named Anna, began a campaign to remember the life work of her mother. It is said that young Anna remembered a Sunday school lesson that her mother gave in which she said, "I hope and pray that someone, sometime, will found a memorial Mother's Day. There are many days for men, but none for mothers." It was finally in 1914 that Anna's hard work paid off when President Woodrow Wilson signed a bill recognizing Mother's Day as a national holiday.

Initially, people observed Mother's Day by attending church, writing letters to their mothers, and eventually, by sending cards, presents, and flowers. As the commercial gift-giving activity associated with Mother's Day increased, Anna Jarvis became upset and disillusioned. She believed that the day's sentiment was being ruined by greed and profit. In 1923, she filed a lawsuit to stop a Mother's Day festival, and by the time of her death in 1948, Jarvis is said to have confessed that she regretted ever working to initiate the Mother's Day tradition.

Sympathy still remains for Anna Jarvis' concern that greed and profit have dulled our real care and concern for the role of mothers. Newborns need maternal and paternal bonding, especially, perhaps, the kind of bonding that mothers can provide. Our country, however, on this dimension has shown that it is not concerned with the importance of motherhood or parenting. Out of 193 countries in the United Nations, only a very, very few (4) do not have a national paid parental leave law, and the United States is one of them. And yes, there are twelve weeks of job-guaranteed leave because of the 1993 Family and Medical Leave Act, but it is unpaid and employers with fewer than fifty employees are exempt—and that eliminates a large percentage of workers. As of 2023, only 24 percent of US private sector workers got any paid family leave, according to the Bureau of Labor Statistics. We surely have not put our money where our mouths are. Imagine! At the very bottom of the pack in the world when it comes to providing paid leave for maternity and parenting responsibilities that we affirm to be of superior importance.

I am reminded, however, of the sainted American humorist, Will Rogers, who said that "there is nothing as easy as denouncing ... It don't take much to see that something is wrong, but it does take some eyesight to see what will put it right again." So think about "putting it right" by voting for our representatives who support some of the most important values in our culture, including children and child rearing, and encourage them to quit prioritizing war, corporate welfare, tax breaks for the top 1 percent, and the most expensive healthcare system in the world—as a few examples. This year as we celebrate our mothers, remember what an unknown author said, namely: "Life doesn't come with a manual, it comes with a mother."

APRIL FOOLS' DAY THOUGHTS

The history of April Fools' Day is uncertain, but the name of it calls us to reflect on one aspect of our shared humanity. Mark Twain, for example, defined April 1 as "….the day upon which we are reminded of what we are on the other three hundred and sixty-four." What is it that we are "the other three hundred and sixty-four"? As a noun, the word "fool" identifies a person who acts silly, unwisely, or imprudently. As a verb, it means to dupe, trick, or deceive someone. As an adjective, it describes someone as silly or foolish. However one decides to use the descriptor "fool," it is not something we usually wish to have applied to us.

As we reflect on this approaching and otherwise "silly" day, I propose that we reflect on Twain's comment about our human propensity toward foolish behavior. I think the best summary of such behavior I have ever come across is contained in an ancient Arabian proverb by an anonymous author. It says that *a fool may be known by six things: anger without cause; speech without profit; change without progress; inquiry without object; putting trust in a stranger; and mistaking foes for friends.*

After using a part of April Fools' Day to pull the best trick ever on your spouse, child, or friend, it may also be good to reflect on the quoted six ways in which we all can act foolish sometimes:

1. Becoming angry for no good reason. (The negative effects both mentally and physically are well documented)
2. Saying things that produce negative instead of positive results. (The first divides us from others, the second enhances our relationships with others)
3. Supporting changes that damage the future good of all instead of improving it. (Think of the current discussion on climate change, unequal distribution of wealth, healthcare etc.)
4. Raising critical questions without investing the time and effort in the critical inquiry needed to provide solutions. (It is easy to complain and denigrate, time-consuming to seek the objective "truths" about the issue, and sometimes challenging to share the outcome of such inquiry)
5. Believing what we read, hear, or watch without doing due diligence on the source and the content. (There are numerous and easily available non-partisan independent news-rating organizations that can help you determine the level of truthfulness and accuracy.)

William Penn provided some tried and true ways in which to sort out those who are foes and those who are friends. He said *that "a true friend accepts freely, advises justly, assists readily, adventures boldly, takes all patiently, defends courageously, and continues a friend unchangeably."* We are entering a season of political promises again. Listen carefully, check records, analyze results, and pick your "friends" very carefully in terms of Penn's definition – not only in politics but in real life.

GOOD TROUBLE?

As a culture, the USA has just celebrated the life of John Lewis, the civil rights advocate, and long-term US representative. He often told of his mother reminding him to stay out of trouble. As he matured in life and experience, he came to differentiate between bad trouble and good trouble. He became memorable for avoiding bad trouble and demonstrating the change that can take place through involving oneself in good trouble. Based upon his life and his behaviors, he apparently believed that conflicts between humans could best be resolved without force or violence. He often noted that using violence to "resolve" conflict means that one party loses or is forced to give up while the other party wins. Under those circumstances, both parties lose.

He showed and reminded us that in almost all of our human relationships, we use nonviolent methods most of the time. What a bigger mess we would be in if we didn't. Think of how it would be if we used violence instead of negotiation each time we wanted what someone else had? Or if we used violence every time someone angered or obstructed us? You can see why we use nonviolent behaviors and methods in most of our family and other disagreements. We use them at work, at school, and in our daily commercial trading activities. We use them in almost all of our relationships between communities within the borders of nations, and in most relations between the various nations. In reality, most of us never explicitly use violence at all. A few may resort to it only in occasional situations.

At this troublesome time during a period of transition in our society, John Lewis's legacy reminds us that most of us are believers in and practitioners of nonviolence in our human relationships. Our daily and unified challenge is to broaden our beliefs and skills to the more difficult situations of human conflict. John Lewis's life demonstrated that those who really commit themselves to nonviolent principles find that they work. Lives are saved, destruction and heartache are avoided, and everyone benefits as the process develops. Politicians and others often tell us that it is impossible to resolve conflicts without the violence of war. History provides ample evidence that leaders often don't try hard enough to resolve conflicts through nonviolence. The result is that it is our lives and our well-being that they put on the line when they decide that violence is necessary.

With the death of John Lewis, the struggles of our country show their persistence over time. The struggles continue between the forces of hope and fear, justice and authoritarianism, love and hatred. Those who are inspired by Lewis are reinvigorated; those who disagree with his words and examples are also now revitalized. Some call Lewis a hero. A hero is not a person who can do things that no one else can do. A hero is someone whose love and faith and endurance jolt and shake the rest of us out of our apathy and inaction just enough to imagine that each of us is capable of doing similar things.

A commitment to nonviolent behavior still leaves a lot of room to get into trouble. As Lewis said, "When you see something that is not right, not fair, not just, you have to stand up, speak up, speak out, and find a way to get in the way and get in trouble. Good trouble. Necessary trouble."

INTERNATIONAL WOMEN'S DAY
IS FOR MEN

March 8 is International Women's Day. The theme for this year is "Embrace Equity," suggesting we all work harder in challenging gender stereotypes, in calling out discrimination, in drawing attention to biases, and in promoting inclusion. Established in 1909, International Women's Day now provides an annual opportunity to report progress on women's rights. While much has changed for the better in the intervening 114 years, the UN Development Forum gender index still finds that 90 percent of the population in seventy-five countries is biased against women.

About thirty years ago, men's rights activists, reacting to what they considered to be unfair custody rights, began to talk about gynocentrism (dominated by or emphasizing feminine interests or a feminine point of view) and its efforts to undermine the rights of men. Some activists see rights as a zero-sum game. In other words, it is as if there exists only a limited pool of rights, and if women gain more, then men must inevitably have less. Some call this a "war on masculinity." There's even an International Men's Day (Nov. 19).

I would note that men's lives often are not that great. The global reality of a higher rate of male suicide attests to that. The cause, however, is not related to women's rights but to the way that masculinity has been defined and constituted in patriarchal cultures. Patriarchal societies damage not just women but also men.

The zero-sum idea that women's rights are gained at the expense of men's rights, however, is the opposite of the empirical truth. A recent World Health Organization report, for example, found that "men benefit from living in more gender-equal societies and that policies promoting gender equality improve the quality of life of everyone, not just for women." More specifically, in societies with more gender-equal perspectives, men are less likely to commit suicide, are half as likely to be depressed, have around a 40 percent smaller risk of dying a violent death, and even suffer less from chronic back pain. Adolescent boys in those countries, too, have fewer psychosomatic complaints and are more likely to use contraceptives.

So how far have women come in the last 114 years? While today's public debates around gender fluidity and #MeToo would have unthinkable a few decades ago, today's realities would conversely have shocked us. Rape numbers have soared, a fifty-year-old Constitutional protection of women's reproductive rights has been eliminated, and the Equal Rights Amendment, while passed by the requisite number of states, has still not been implemented.

We males could all move to Iceland where the men have the highest life expectancy in Europe, due not, I think, to the cold weather and herring, but to the smallest economic and social gender gap than any other country. More likely and effective, however, would be for more men to join campaigns for gender equality. Why? It would not only signal that we're the good guys, or be morally just, but it is also in our enlightened self-interest to do so. It is good for us!

CONFLICTED BEGINNINGS –
HOPEFUL EXPECTATIONS

As our calendar year always seems to speed to a close, it remains a marvel that our species ability to disagree about almost everything does not seem to affect our ability to survive. For example, the disagreement about when the old year ends and the new year begins. The first known new year celebrations began about 2000 BC in Mesopotamia (in present-day Iraq, lying between the Tigris and Euphrates Rivers). It occurred at the vernal equinox, toward the end of March. The Babylonians, then living in the region, had a religious festival named Akitu (barley). The festival would last for eleven days and marked the time that Marduk, Babylon's sky god, defeated Tiamat, the evil sea goddess.

In the same time period, the new year for Persians, Egyptians, and Phoenicians started in the fall equinox, while the Greeks celebrated the new year during the winter solstice. Then, around 753 BC, the first Roman calendar arrived with 10 months or 304 days only, making March 1 the beginning of a new year. The new year became January 1 by 46 BC, when Julius Caesar developed the solar-based Julian calendar because the old lunar-based Roman calendar had become ineffective. A final change came in 1582 when Pope Gregory XIII implemented the Gregorian calendar in Rome. Minimal changes were applied to the Roman (Julian) calendar. The Catholic church first followed the Gregorian calendar, which was then slowly adopted by European countries like Germany, Denmark, Russia, and Scotland. Today, the Gregorian calendar is the one we still use.

We are about to complete the year 2023 on the Gregorian calendar. We have experienced the invasion of Ukraine, the many mass shootings including school shootings, numerous storms, tornadoes and hurricanes, another election, inflation, COVID, RSV, and flu! The words of T.S. Eliot come to mind: "For last year's words belong to last year's language, and next year's words await another voice." That voice is summarized in the words of Alfred Lord Tennyson. He says that "hope smiles from the threshold of the year to come, whispering 'it will be happier.'" Hope is often our first conscious emotion in a new year, and it may also be yours. Surely, the coming year will have a beginning, a middle, and an end. It is usually hope that plays a different but vital role at all these stages. It is hope that often sets our to-do list for the coming year. Our resolutions become articulated hopes for how our lives will improve. Hope—the most powerful driving force for change.

By the end of 2024, we will have let some hopes go, some will have been fulfilled, and others will still be works in progress. But by then, we will again be having new hopes, little seedlings of hope to start the whole process over again. Through it all, may we live with undaunted hope, enduring trust, and unreserved love.

SECTION II

COMMON SENSE THINKING ABOUT THE GOVERNMENT

gov·ern·ment ˈgə-vər(n)-mənt : the body of persons that constitutes the governing authority of a political unit or organization: such as the officials comprising the governing body of a political unit and constituting the organization as an active agency.

PROPOSING A PURPLE REIGN

We are living in a time of political mischief, much of it malicious. Perhaps that's why our first President, George Washington, offered these comments about such behavior: "The common and continual mischiefs of the spirit of [political] party are sufficient to make it the interest and duty of a wise people to discourage and restrain it," and "[The spirit of party] serves always to distract the public councils and enfeeble the public administration. It agitates the community with ill-founded jealousies and false alarms, [and] kindles the animosity of one party against another." After over 247 years, things seem not to have changed. What, if anything, can we do?

First, a short note about definitions. Unfortunately, our country has been divided into reds (conservatives) and blues (liberals). Defining the terms by their root meanings, the word *conservative* comes from a derivation of the eleventh century Old English word *cunnen*, which came to be shortened to *con*. It also comes from the Proto-Indo-European root word *ser*. *Con* means "to make an attempt, try or seek to do," while *ser* means "to protect." So the root meaning of *conservative* is someone "seeking to protect the status quo." The word *liberal* comes from the Latin word *liber*, which means "pertaining to or befitting a free person" and "free, unrestricted, unimpeded." So the root meaning of *liberal* is someone seeking "the freedom to initiate change."

Let's assume conservatives (red) and liberals (blue) each have their roles to play. Let's recognize and affirm that conservatives (those generally predisposed to resist change) have an important place in society. Humans, cross-culturally, seem to be predominantly resistant to change and most comfortable with the status quo. That being the case, most likely conservatives are not now, never have been, nor ever will be an endangered species. In fact, the difficulty with getting any social movement or social change accomplished is that most people do not want to be moved or changed!

So we might agree that this comfort with the status quo is not inherently bad. Without it, sociologists tell us that there would be insufficient social organization for an orderly society. Without a majority of people wanting to stay put where they are and keep working as they are, the consequent social change would likely lead to more social disorganization than a society could long endure. In short, we need conservatives and can appreciate the social stability they bring to our culture.

But we also need liberals (those generally predisposed to freely encourage and support change) to balance, to challenge, and to inspire those who are comfortable with things as they are. Liberals almost always constitute a minority for the reason mentioned above. Liberals constitute a continuing "endangered species" because their disposition toward change confounds the majority, frightens some, worries many, and often challenges predominant societal assumptions. It may be easier not to have liberals around, but without their balance and impetus toward change, social life would stagnate.

What can we do? We can agree that most people have some of both traditional conservatism and liberalism woven within their personal and world views. Most of the people around us are neither totally "red" nor totally "blue" in the sense of current political identification. Rather, we see them in varying shades of purple (that wonderful mix of red and blue). Perhaps we can start to see that most of us are somewhere on the purple spectrum. We can also recognize that we share some common values about the conflicted issues of the day. What we are not very good at is simply speaking to one another to find those common values that can draw us together. It is always time to try.

A TEST OF CHARACTER

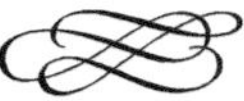

It was Abraham Lincoln who said, "Nearly all men can stand adversity, but if you want to test a man's character, give him power." With regard to human behavior, *power* is often defined as the ability to coerce someone to do something, even against their will. *Character* usually refers to the moral and ethical qualities of a person. If Lincoln was correct, the biggest challenge to a person's moral and ethical qualities is having and exercising power. Add to that the current concern about how few people in our country hold so much power to exert their will on the many (who feel and increasingly are powerless), and one can feel the depth of unrest in our country.

I am delighted, therefore, that the public is being introduced to a political theory developed by sociologist Robert Michels in 1911. He called it the "iron law of oligarchy," and it predicts that rule by an elite, or oligarchy, is the inevitable outcome within any democratic organization. Specifically, he suggests that even representational democracies, such as ours, will inevitably succumb to rule by an elite few (an oligarchy). To this apparent tendency toward the rule of a few, add money and diminishing moral and ethical character, and we can see why we can get leaders who in many cases were neither elected by popular vote nor by a non-gerrymandered representational vote.

Specifically, some of our recent Presidents did not receive the majority of the votes cast, and a recent US House majority held 57 percent of the seats while receiving only 52 percent of the votes.

So we are living in an unfortunate circular conundrum: money buys power, power rewards the monied, and together they pursue the interests of the few to the neglect of the many. The sainted comedian, George Carlin, said this of what he felt had become of the American dream: "It's called the American dream because you have to be asleep to believe it." So now what?

How about considering an alternative to the "iron law of oligarchy"? We might want to call it the "Iron Law of Character." This "law" would operate out of the general perspective that political and corporate power must always be held in check by the superior power of social responsibility in order for a democracy to be maintained. Social responsibility, in this case, means putting people before profit and a sustainable planet before the pillaging of it, and prioritizing the general welfare of both as a summary of the common good. Why? Because right now a very small handful of wealthy and powerful families and corporations control the destiny of our nation and much of our world. Too many people, from the very beginning of this country, have struggled and died to maintain our democratic vision. We owe it to them and to our children to continue to maintain it.

May we be inspired, encouraged, and energized to do just that by the words of Frederick Douglass (1818–1895), who was a famed author and orator, an eminent human rights leader in the anti-slavery movement, and the first African American citizen to hold a high US government rank. "If there is no struggle, there is no progress. ... This struggle may be a moral one; or it may be a physical one; or it may be both moral and physical; but it must be a struggle. Power concedes nothing without a demand. It never did and it never will." May the power of renewed social responsibility lead us also to a renewal of our democratic vision: to re-create a civil society in which active and informed citizens are dominant and together make policy decisions based on the will of the majority and accomplishing a shared common good.

WHY ARE WE INTERESTED IN CIVIL BEHAVIOR?

While uncivil behavior has a long history within human cultures, the arch toward greater civility in secular, political, and public affairs seemed to be increasing in our own culture until about fifty years ago. It began to change, in my memory and judgment, when division and vilification of the opposite political party became the new norm in our Congress. It was also a time when the very role of government was questioned, negatively defined, and publicly excoriated. In the next five decades, civics courses in our public schools declined and were eliminated, "common good" safety nets were constantly challenged and removed, and public discourse became increasingly angry. So here we now are, divided, untrusting, angry, and often uncivil with others.

In Latin, the roots of two related words, *civis* (citizen) and *civita* (city), reflect the connection necessary for civil behavior as a means of maintaining a functioning society. Together, they provide a code of social behaviors that create order and provide for the common good of all citizens. In other words, civility is simply "decency" and "being considerate of others" in all interpersonal relationships.

Our first President, George Washington, was likely being disciplined in elementary school by being told to copy a sixteenth century set of behavioral rules compiled for young people by Jesuits. They are still available as "The 110 Rules of Civil Behavior." They ended up being one of the earliest and most effective forces to shape the life of our first President. They were designed to help form our inner habits by shaping our outer habits. In other words, we become the kind of people on the inside that we learn to act like on the outside. To become civil, we need to learn to be and act civil.

THOUGHTS ABOUT PRESIDENTS' DAY

We are about to celebrate another Presidents' Day on the third Monday in February (the 21st this year). This occasion was originally celebrated in 1885 in recognition of President George Washington. While it was first celebrated on February 22, Washington's actual day of birth, the holiday became popularly known as Presidents' Day after it was moved as part of 1971's Uniform Monday Holiday Act. That Act was an attempt to create more three-day weekends for our nation's workers. While several states still have individual holidays honoring the birthdays of Washington, Abraham Lincoln, and other figures, Presidents' Day is now popularly viewed as a day to celebrate all U.S. Presidents, past and present.

It has always been my understanding that the office of the President, no matter who sits in the oval office, deserves our respect. Therefore, we need to be very careful about belittling the office through excessive partisan activity because in doing so, we lessen the authority that the office deserves as one of the three branches of our government. The President of the United States is our leader, our chief executive, the person who the rest of the world looks to as representing all of us, the people of the United States. Not only do we rightfully expect a President to provide decisive leadership in times of crisis, but they must also demonstrate compassion and determination to bind up our nation's wounds and demonstrate dignity for the office and for all people.

As has been particularly evident these past few years, some presidents are more successful than others, some are more honest, and some are more informed and interested in using the role for the common good. For those interested, there is ample public information available that rates all of our presidents. In our current political climate, however, one can wonder just how far partisanship can be displayed before it becomes demeaning to the office. Has our political system become so infected with partisan rancor, that what is best for the country becomes less important than partisan gain? The phrase "the loyal opposition" is important to consider, in that it implies that a person from the opposition party is still loyal to their oath and to their nation. That loyalty, of course, encourages open and honest discourse about opposing ideas and issues, but always in a civil, informed, and courteous manner. It does sometimes seem as if that is no longer the norm, and anything is fair game when dealing with our President and family. Is it okay to lie about them? Is it okay to personally attack the spouse of the President, or their children, or even their pets? What are the limitations these days to how we treat not only our President but all of our civic leaders, including those in Hudson?

Already as a child, I was taught that it was proper to use the phrase, Mr. President, or at least to always say "President" and then the person's last name. It is just good manners and a matter of respect. I don't know about you, but I don't like any stranger to call me by my last name, without a Mr. or some other appropriate title in front of it. It is just rude. As one of my favorite common philosophers, the longshoreman Eric Hoffer, says, "rudeness luxuriates in the absence of self-respect." President's Day is a good day to reflect about how we treat those we have elected to serve us.

THINKING ABOUT PATRIOTISM

Every year we celebrate the July 4, 1776, adoption of the Declaration of Independence, which declared our independence from Great Britain. Nonetheless, once again the patriotism of some of our fellow citizens is being questioned. Whether they are some NFL football players as a new season begins, or former federal intelligence professionals, or citizens of minority status, among others, such questioning provides a teaching moment to review just what it means to be patriotic.

It was Stephen Decatur, a naval officer during the War of 1812, who coined the phrase, "Our country right or wrong." Carl Schurz, a Civil War-era general and senator, said it differently: "Our country, right or wrong; when right to be kept right; when wrong to be set right." These are two patriotic visions. They are both represented in this time of great cultural division about the meaning of patriotism.

Americans, no matter how their views might otherwise differ, can generally agree that a patriot is a person who has an ardent love for his or her country. Nevertheless, despite this common definition, there can be a great divide between people over the issue of how this patriotic devotion is to be expressed. Too often we see and hear people's patriotism being attacked because they hold different views about the meaning of patriotism. This may be due to a misunder-standing about the essence of patriotism.

Rather than patriotism, chauvinism is what many of our fellow citizens currently believe patriotism to be. The word *chauvinism* comes from Nicholas Chauvin, a soldier in Napoleon's army who was blindly loyal to him. Chauvinism is zealous and aggressive patriotism, a conviction that we are better because we are chosen. It expresses itself in excessive enthusiasm for military glory and holds no room for difference of opinion. It is often also expressed as 'exceptionalism." Exceptionalism is a form of ethnocentrism (believing in the superiority of one's group) in that it expresses a belief in the superiority of our nation, which is often believed to be "God-given."

We are a government "of ... by ... and for the people," as Abraham Lincoln said. That means that policies are forged in the public forum as well as in the halls of Congress. To deny differences of opinion and to brand them as unpatriotic is to squelch the very instrument by which democracy lives and breathes. A great tragedy of our time is that open debate is largely lost, and the shrill voices of name-calling and condemnation have taken the place of civility and dialogue.

We are living in difficult and fearful times when well-meaning people, looking to their elected leaders for security, are vulnerable to those who prey on their fears. In such times, chauvinistic policies and attitudes can easily gain ascendancy. Patriotism, for many, has once again become equated with blind acceptance of government leaders and policies. Amid the shouting, wiser and more mature voices have been almost muted, and the noble visions on which America was founded have been distorted, to the detriment of our future viability as a nation. Once again it is time for people and political groups who live by the vision of America's democratic ideals to assert themselves against the destructive policies of the contemporary chauvinists. This is essential as we truly love our country and continue to seek to be "one nation, indivisible, with liberty and justice for all."

GOVERNMENT AND GUNS

I t is my judgement that few cultural changes that have occurred in the past three decades have wreaked more damage than the improper and dishonest changes to the interpretation of our Constitution's Second Amendment. The continuing and consistent mass shootings are primarily due to those changes that now allow almost anyone who breathes and has money to buy exceedingly destructive weapons of war to massacre innocents. Why are we allowing this?

For over two hundred years since the Bill of Rights (the first ten amendments to our Constitution) was adopted in 1791, this amendment remained mostly unnoticed. Adam Winkler (a constitutional law scholar on the faculty of UCLA), in his fairly recent book entitled *Gunfight: The Battle over the Right to Bear Arms in America* (2011, W.W. Norton & Co., NY) reminds the reader that firearms have always been regulated since the beginning of our republic. Over the years, the various laws were hardly challenged, and when they were, the interests of the various states to regulate the ownership and manufacture of firearms were upheld. In summary, judges supported the understanding that the regulation of guns agreed with both common sense and the Second Amendment. For over two hundred years there was consistent agreement.

The actual text of the amendment says, "A well-regulated Militia, being necessary to the security of a free State, the right of the people to keep and bear Arms, shall not be infringed." For over two hundred years the courts held that the first part of the amendment (the militia clause) took precedence over the second part (the bear arms part). The US Supreme Court and the lower courts consistently agreed that this amendment gave state militias the right to bear arms but did not give individuals the right to carry or own a weapon.

So, what changed? In a very brief summary, it was the politics of the NRA, the Congress, and the Supreme Court. The NRA in the 1970s began pushing for a novel interpretation of the Second Amendment that gave individuals, not just militias, the right to bear arms. Initially their views were widely ridiculed. Chief Justice Warren E. Burger, a conservative jurist, mocked the individual-rights theory of the amendment as "a fraud." But by 2008, after several Republican-controlled Congresses had been able to put in place a majority of conservative Supreme Court justices, that majority won for the Republican Party a long-sought victory in the form of the *District of Columbia* v. *Heller* case. Even to its supporters, this convoluted opinion, penned by the late Justice Antonin Scalia, was noted for its complete and indelible political motivation, the most obvious of any the Supreme Court has issued.

Two years later, conservatives went back to the Supreme Court to also secure the enforcement of an individual right to gun ownership against the states, not just the District of Columbia. In other words, they wanted to limit as much as possible the potential for both federal and state gun control regulation. So finally, in 2016, the political right convinced the Supreme Court conservative majority to formally declare that this new, distorted, and historically unsupported version of the Second Amendment applied equally to all "bearable" arms. Hopefully, wisdom, historical honesty, and informed minds will again predominate.

THE ELEVENTH HOUR OF THE
ELEVENTH DAY OF THE
ELEVENTH MONTH

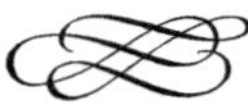

Before our time, it was called Armistice Day. The Cambridge Dictionary defines an armistice as "a formal agreement between two countries or groups at war to stop fighting for a particular time, especially to talk about possible peace." It first commemorated the end of World War I.

I personally applaud any endeavor that talks about possible peace. In this case, such talks precipitated the official ending of World War I when the Treaty of Versailles was signed on June 28, 1919. The fighting, however, had ended about seven months before that, when the Allied Forces and Germany agreed to an armistice on the eleventh hour of the eleventh day of the eleventh month.

That explains why November 11, 1918, was considered the end of "the war to end all wars" and came to be called Armistice Day. It was finally in 1926 that Congress officially recognized it as the end of the war, and in 1938, it became an official holiday to honor veterans of World War I.

As we now know, it was not "the war to end all wars." Soon came World War II and then, shortly after, the Korean War happened. After lobbying by several veterans' organizations, on June 1, 1954, Congress again amended the commemoration by changing the word "armistice" to "veterans" in order to honor American veterans of all wars.

As with all good ideas, someone thought they had a better one. So, the Uniform Holiday Bill (Public Law 90-363 [82 Stat. 250]) was signed on June 28, 1968. The intention was to ensure three-day weekends for Federal employees by celebrating four national holidays on Mondays: Washington's Birthday, Memorial Day, Veterans Day, and Columbus Day. The thinking was that such extended weekends encouraged travel, recreational, and cultural activities, and stimulated greater industrial and commercial production. The many states that did not agree with this decision just continued to celebrate the holidays on their original dates.

It didn't take long for it to become apparent that most US citizens wanted to celebrate Veterans Day on Nov. 11, since it was a matter of historic and patriotic significance. So once again another idea prevailed when on September 20, 1975, President Gerald Ford signed another law (Public Law 94-97 [89 Stat. 479]), which in 1978 returned the annual observance to its original date.

Inasmuch as World War I was a multinational effort, it made sense that our allies also wanted to celebrate their veterans on November 11. Both Canada and Australia call November 11 "Remembrance Day." Many Canadian citizens wear red poppy flowers based on the poem "In Flanders Fields" (but that is another story) to honor their war dead. Some in the USA do the same. In Australia, the day is similar to our Memorial Day.

Veterans Day honors all who have served our country in war or peace, dead or living, although it's mostly intended to thank living veterans for their sacrifices. The words of former President Obama are a good reminder to us: "It's about how we treat our veterans every single day of the year. It's about making sure they have the care they need and the benefits that they've earned when they come home. It's about serving all of you as well as you've served the United States of America."

PEACE OFFICERS? RETHINKING A NAME

Many times during the past year, the regional and national news reports have caused folks to reflect more on police activities. Someplace in that process, some wondered how we went from "peace" officers to "police" officers. My memory as a child growing up in a small town in Iowa was knowing that our one officer was called a peace officer. Does the name we call a social role set expectations for behavior? It was in 2020 that, for the first time since Gallup began tracking public confidence in the police in 1993, a majority of American adults no longer trusted law enforcement.

Maybe the word we use does make a difference. The word *police* dates from about the 1530s and means "the regulation and control of a community." The word *peace*, on the other hand, dates from the mid-twelfth century and means "agreement, treaty of peace, tranquility, or a binding together." The one speaks of regulation and control, and the other seeks agreement, tranquility, and a binding together of all of us.

Were we to use the term peace officer today, it would sound outdated and even antiquated. My guess is that most people reading this who are under forty have never heard the term actually used by anyone. To them, we might as well be talking about floppy disks or even buggy whips. But from the 1800s through the 1960s, the term was widely used in our country to refer generally to law officers, including sheriffs, troopers, marshals, and the lowly constables. Today the old title "peace officer" has been virtually eliminated in popular usage, typically replaced by "police officer" or the more recent "law enforcement officer."

The stereotype of a peace officer is mostly fiction. The sheriffs we often see in westerns are portrayed as stern lawmen carrying Colt revolvers called "Peacemakers." But it may be good to remember that the Wyatt Earps of western movie myth weren't always so peaceful and, often, at least in movies, used their Peacemakers to shoot up the place and disturb the peace. In a slightly more recent historical setting, Sheriff Andy Taylor of the *Andy Griffith Show* is likely the most memorable example of what "peace officer" once meant, at least in the American subconscious. The TV show was, of course, fictional, and unfortunately there have been many small-town sheriffs in America over the past and current decades that have been anything but peace officers. Yet, it is a good reminder that just a few decades ago Americans could identify with the character of Sheriff Taylor as a recognizable ideal "peace officer."

The situation today is quite different. Police have experienced a serious decline over the last several decades in their public image, and many more average citizens now often fear police officers rather than trust them. This is especially true among poor and minority communities who have been less trusting (and maybe less naïve) about their experiences with police. But today, a similar view has found its way into middle-class awareness. Trying to address the many and complex causes of this cultural attitude shift is beyond the scope of this brief viewpoint. One wonders, however, if we would remove the huge word "police" that now fills the height and width of both sides and backs of our cities' vehicles and replace that word with the city logo and the words "peace officer," we might gently begin the process of defining their role as being responsible for "seeking agreement, tranquility, and a binding together of all of us."

RESCIND THE SECOND AMENDMENT

Unsuspecting and innocent children have again been murdered while in school. Nineteen second, third, and fourth graders. And two teachers. Uvalde, Texas. Adjectives describing these continuing killings escape me. Emotions concerning gun ownership and use, and those who encourage and support them, are difficult to keep in check.

What do we do? America has more guns than any other nation in the world, 393 million or 120 for every 100 citizens. That is double that of the next highest nation and compares with one gun per every seven people worldwide. We are about 4 percent of the world's population and own about one third of all the guns. Thirty-two percent of Americans own a gun (68 percent do not). "Shameful" may be one descriptive adjective to describe our cultural reality about guns.

What do we do? Let's rescind the Second Amendment. It has happened before, when the Twenty-First Amendment repealed prohibition in the Eighteenth, and it seems essential to accomplish it again. I still agree with the former conservative Chief Justice Warren Burger in 1991: "If I were writing the Bill of Rights now, there wouldn't be any such thing as the Second Amendment." He continued, "The right of the people to keep and bear arms" was the subject of "one of the greatest pieces of fraud – I repeat the word 'fraud' – on the American public by special-interest groups that I have ever seen in my lifetime."

Sometimes our historical honesty requires us to acknowledge that the Founders and the Constitution made some mistakes. This is one of those times. The Second Amendment must be rescinded—repealed. The Twelfth Amendment changed one mistake, the Twenty-First another. And then there were the changes about race and slavery, women's suffrage, and presidential succession, among others. The Second Amendment is outdated and a threat to safety and liberty. When it was adopted in 1791, there were no weapons remotely like the assault rifle, the word "bullet" did not exist, and many of the advances of modern weaponry were not yet even invented or popularized. When the Second Amendment was written, the Founders didn't have to weigh the risks of one person killing nineteen children all by himself. Now we do, and the risk-benefit analysis of 1791 is irrelevant to the risk-benefit analysis of today.

And as for liberty, it is not a one-way street. It also includes the liberty to send your child to school so that they can begin to be filled with a love of learning. And, of course, the liberty to go to a movie, to your religious house of worship, to the supermarket, or anywhere, and still feel that you are free to do so without thinking about the risk of being gunned down by someone brandishing a weapon that can easily kill you and countless others. The liberty of the minority to own guns cannot supersede the liberty of everyone else to live their lives free from the risk of being easily murdered. It has for too long, too many innocents have suffered, and it is time to say, "No more."

BLESSED ARE THE RESTLESS

A major election season again! It started too early. It's been taking too long. It's costing too much. It's divisive and too negative. "I am a restless soul, hungry, perhaps wretched," said Bob Dylan. Thomas Edison tempered my restlessness a bit by saying that "restlessness is discontent, and discontent is the first necessity of progress. Show me a thoroughly satisfied person and I will show you a failure."

I confess to being restless and discontented about trying to be an active participant in the kind of self-government our form of representative democracy used to exhibit. I have more and more come to think that many of us are now reduced to being passive spectators who are less likely to bother with politics, because a class of professional technicians has taken charge of electoral politics. These professionals (including campaign managers, pollsters, pundits, advertisers, and fundraisers, to mention a few examples) have come to manage both the passions and the passivity of voters like us. They predominantly shape the content of what we know as well as what we do not know.

The manner in which we voters are manipulated costs a huge sum of money, mostly paid for by private donations. These private donors, often business and corporate donors, then expect to influence the content of the public political messages, meaning that campaigns are almost always biased in favor of the interests of the rich and powerful. The result is that the purpose of campaigns has now changed from educating citizens to electing or defeating certain politicians. In my judgment, this is a primary reason that the current "largest political party" is made up of those eighty million potential voters who stay at home and do not vote. Of those who did vote in the last general election, Gallup reported that 46 percent of those surveyed identified as independents, 28 percent identified as Democrats, and 24 percent as Republicans.

This may also be the reason that so many potential voters seem so angry these days. Regardless of their ideological or partisan perspectives, many have come to believe that our senators and representatives, on both state and federal levels, have not worked together to bring us the consensus changes on which huge majorities agree. They have failed to hear the messages so often shared by their constituents. For example, we have just witnessed another brutal mass killing at an elementary school in Uvalde, Texas, even as a large majority of Americans desire greater control of gun sales and use. In other words, our elected officials are seen as distancing themselves from the common-sense and popular knowledge of ordinary folks like us.

But the following may be the good news. We are already significantly involved in a new era, a generational shift of younger voters and elected officials who are demanding change on consensus issues. They are also using democratizing technologies that offer better power to control communications. While this ability has been used for divisive purposes as well as for consensus building, it is well into destabilizing the old way of doing politics. I think it is a major factor in generating the many unexpected turns of this election season. It is reducing the cost of making political connections (especially financial), and the time and work to organize across long distances and social divisions. It even seems to be the beginning of diluting the political domination of the 1 percent, the corporations, and billion-aires. All I can say is blessed are the restless. May they (hopefully, we) continue to bring about meaningful and positive unrest.

LOW TURNOUT EQUALS POOR GOVERNMENT

We are quickly approaching the 2024 USA elections. While there is some disagreement about the extent of voter turnout and whether or not it is declining, the reality remains that even in good turnout years, many of our eligible voters simply neglect to vote. There are many empirically derived reasons for this fact, but those reasons, in my opinion, pale before the reasons we all should take the time to vote on the first Tuesday in November. Here are some of them:

First, and most of all, this is YOUR country, a constitutional republic that can only work as intended if you register and vote.

Second, it's YOUR money! It is our city council, our county commissioners, our governor, our state officials and legislators, our president, and members of Congress that YOU vote for who will decide how much of our public wealth to invest in public services and how to fairly share the tax burden.

Third, they are OUR children and OUR neighborhoods. We want to do the best to keep our children healthy, fed, safe, cared for, and educated; and it is the officials that WE elect who will set the policies for families pursuing their hopes and dreams. So also with our neighborhoods. WE elect officials and judges that make daily decisions about crime prevention, laws and law enforcement, safe and affordable homes, traffic patterns, and where to put schools, parks, and recreation.

Finally, WE elect the people who make the decisions about our jobs, our highways, our healthcare, and our Social Security.

In short, we receive the quality of government we deserve. If we do not vote, we simply do not have the right to complain about the leadership on any level of government. If we do vote without first learning about the candidates and the values they have demonstrated, we are only slightly better than those who do not vote at all. As the saying goes, "Garbage in, garbage out." As you prepare for this important election, I would encourage you to check out http://www.votesmart.org. I know how hard it is in these times of extreme partisan division to trust any organization. Nonetheless, I encourage you to check out their website and, if you are as convinced of their nonpartisan perspective as I am, use their tools before you vote to learn about all the candidates that are important to you. Then please vote!

THE DUTY OF YOUTH

The Scottish philosopher, David Hume, reminded us that "the corruption of the best things gives rise to the worst." David Hume died in the year our country was founded, but his words are still both prescient and cautionary for us. During this election season, the accusations of corruption seem to fly more easily and regularly. The word *corruption* comes from a Middle English word *corrupcio* (1300-1350), and is typically defined as illegal or dishonest behaviors, especially by those who hold positions of power and show impairment of moral virtues, principles, or values.

While corruption can have a much broader application, it is corruption in our government at all levels that is often forced to the forefront of our thinking. It emanates from Washington, D.C., through all the states, and into our own local communities. It impacts all the citizens that elected, appointed, and employed officials were and are supposed to serve and protect. But an even more specific type of corruption holds our attention. While government corruption may be broken down into political corruption, judicial corruption, and police corruption, it currently is political corruption that challenges our Constitutional principles and is of broad public concern.

One of the challenges involves the continuing attention on the elections process. Claims that the 2020 election was fraudulent have been soundly and repeatedly disproven through exhaustive audits, recounts, reports, and reviews. Most of our fellow citizens agree, but about 35 percent still believe the election was fraudulent. This percentage has remained stable since November 2020. Repeated claims of corruption when it does not exist is also a form of corruption that breeds distrust and chaos, as January 6, 2021, has shown.

More commonly, political corruption comes in the form of manipulating policies to the advantage of the monied and powerful. It can also accompany the instituting of new rules and procedures or changing long-held and majority-approved rules. It often shows itself in the allocation of funding or other resources. In short, it is abusing a position of authority to increase or maintain the power, status, or wealth of a group or individual.

So, what can we do? The American humorist, Will Rogers, said that "it is awful hard to get people interested in corruption unless they can get some of it." There are ways to prove Will Rogers wrong. To summarize the volumes of information available about addressing corruption, the four following responses can be helpful.

First, end impunity. The research demonstrates that the most effective way to reduce corruption among public officials is to break the cycle of impunity, or freedom from punishment or loss, and ensure the corrupt are punished. This requires a strong legal framework, law enforcement, and an independent and effective court system.

Second, corruption can be reduced by improving public confidence in financial management, disclosing budget information which prevents waste and misappropriation of resources, and providing communities easy opportunities to comment on the proposed budgets of their local government.

Third, corruption is reduced if there is government openness, freedom of the press, transparency, and access to information. It is especially the access to information aspect that increases the responsiveness of government bodies, while also having a positive effect on the levels of public participation.

Finally, empowering citizens to peacefully hold government accountable is a sustainable approach to reducing corruption. I remember when Kurt Cobain said that "the duty of youth is to challenge corruption." His reminder applies to us all.

GRIDLOCK ABOUT MEMORIAL DAY?

Each year we celebrate Memorial Day on the last Monday in May. When I was a kid, we called it "Decoration Day," because gravesites of veterans who died in our nation's service were decorated. While there are many different stories about how this patriotic holiday originated, everyone seems to agree on the following: the day was officially proclaimed on May 5, 1868, by General John Logan, national commander of the Grand Army of the Republic, and was first observed on May 30, 1868, when flowers were placed on the graves of Union and Confederate soldiers at Arlington National Cemetery. By 1890 it was recognized by all of the northern states. The southern states honored their dead on separate days until after World War I (when the holiday changed from honoring just those who died fighting in the Civil War to honoring Americans who died fighting in any war).

So what about "gridlock"? Memorial Day is now celebrated on the last Monday in May (passed by Congress with the National Holiday Act of 1971 [P.L. 90-363] to ensure a three-day weekend for Federal holidays). There are some, however, who feel that when Congress made the day into a three-day weekend, it became easier for people to be distracted from the spirit and meaning of the day. The VFW, for example, said that "changing the date merely to create three-day weekends has undermined the very meaning of the day. No doubt, this has contributed greatly to the general public's nonchalant observance of Memorial Day."

Here is where we are now on that issue: on January 19, 1999, the sainted senator from Hawaii, Daniel Inouye, introduced Senate Bill 189, which proposes to restore the traditional day of observance of Memorial Day back to May 30 instead of "the last Monday in May." On April 19, 1999, the sainted Representative Sam Gibbons introduced the bill to the House (H.R. 1474). The bills were referred to the Committee on the Judiciary and the Committee on Government Reform. To date, there have been no further developments on them. For us, being "nonchalant" about the sacrifices of so many on behalf of our country is not who we are. We join you in saying a hearty "THANKS" to all those who have served on our behalf.

GRACE AND MERCY

I recently heard these definitions while in church: "Grace is receiving something you don't deserve," and "mercy is not receiving something you do deserve." I have been thinking about these words since. Our country is gravely divided. Our political leadership on the federal level and, often, also on the state level are leading the charge of dividing citizen against citizen, most often based upon race, religion, or ethnicity. This is not new in our culture. What is fairly new is the level of anger and hatred that often accompany such division. Also, for about the past forty years, increasing political partisanship has infected human relationships. To some degree, all, and each of us, are participants in this downward spiraling and evil process.

Unless you are Native American, a descendent of a slave, or a first-generation immigrant, you are here as a descendent of an immigrant. You had nothing to do with it and have no inherent right to the benefit of it. In short, you are here by grace – receiving something you don't deserve. In my own case, my paternal grandfather came, as a teenager, to the USA as an indentured servant, according to census records. My benefits from his risks and hard work are undeserved. They are a gift. My guess is that you also have similar stories.

And then there is mercy. Reflecting upon the many times in our personal, familial, and national lives in which we know we truly deserved to be held accountable but weren't, we are reminded that mercy in its root meaning is forgiveness. And when we receive mercy instead of accountability, we are quite literally changed from the inside out. Mercy matters, both in receiving it and in giving it. It matters because we all need mercy from time to time, but it also matters because giving it is what can unite us in spite of our differences. Mercy in these days can be demonstrated by one's openness to those with whom one might strongly disagree. While not ending there, mercy begins with such small acts of understanding, which can lead to life-changing experiences of understanding, care, and even love.

And speaking of grace and mercy, Ronald Reagan, in his last speech as president, quoted a letter from a man who told him: "'You can go to live in France, but you cannot become a Frenchman. You can go to live in Germany or Turkey or Japan, but you cannot become a German, a Turk, or a Japanese. But anyone, from any corner of the Earth, can come to live in America and become an American.'" After reading the letter, Reagan said it summarized what "is one of the most important sources of America's greatness. We lead the world because, unique among nations, we draw our people—our strength—from every country and every corner of the world." We are here by grace, we remain here by mercy, and we affirm our diversity as the strength of our unity.

AN APOTHEGM OF HISTORICAL IMPORT

According to the Merriam-Webster Dictionary, an apothegm is "a short, pithy, and instructive saying or formulation." Here is an apothegm that calls for reflective thought in these times: "The ends justify the means." To most people who use the expression, it is often an excuse for achieving their goals through whatever means are necessary, no matter how illegal, immoral, or disgusting the means may be. It is really saying that it doesn't matter how you get what you want as long as you get what you want. It usually involves doing something wrong in order to achieve what is seen as a positive end, and then justifying the wrongdoing by identifying the "good" outcome.

The idea that any means can be justified by an appropriate end has been discredited throughout human history. The major religions decry it. All major ethical philosophers, from Socrates and Plato to Hume and Kant, universally reject it. And at our country's beginning, our politicians rejected it. In the winter of 1777, George Washington chose to encamp at Valley Forge. His eleven thousand troops were hungry, sick, poorly clothed, cold, and wet. If he had followed the tradition of warfare throughout human history, he would have taken by force from area farms the provisions necessary to support his troops. But he did not do so because he lacked legal authority for such actions.

Instead, his troops suffered deprivation because Washington knew something that many current political leaders do not: the ends do not justify the means. He did not succumb to convenience or invoke national security to take illegal actions but chose instead to send repeated requests to the Continental Congress for the legal authority to do so. He did not hear back in a timely fashion, and unfortunately many soldiers died. Nonetheless, if anybody could have ever reasonably invoked the idea that the end justifies the means, Washington would have been that man. Because he believed so firmly in the value of laws in a struggling new nation based upon the principles of inalienable rights for its citizens, he did not.

From that time to the present moment, when we have acted upon the corrupt idea that ends justify the means, nothing seems to have constrained our basest instincts. In politics, we have ended up with Japanese detention camps, witch hunts for "communists" by the House Un-American Activities Committee, illegal wiretapping, falsified evidence for war and torture, the separation from parents and incarceration of children, extreme gerrymandering, and the voting disenfranchisement of groups of people. In business, the financial recession of 2008-2009 can be summed up as a group of investment bankers who sought to become millionaires by trading in subprime mortgages, knowing the homeowner might never make the payments but not worrying about it since the bankers sold off those mortgages to third parties who then assumed the risk. They manipulated the means to achieve their ends. These are just a few examples of gross and callous disregard for law that George Washington fought specifically to prevent.

One more point. We now have in our country two almost opposite definitions for the word *principle*. For many, being principled means honoring procedures and laws (means) as the core of civil behavior. For others, it means fighting for the desired outcome (ends) even at the expense of procedural and legal niceties. In short, the principle of defining *achieving the ends* as "winning no matter the means it takes to get there," is fraught with historical and current injurious results. Conversely, the principle of honoring procedures and laws is most likely to bring about the ends that serve the needs of most of us. Two quick quotes in closing from political descendants of Washington: it was Abraham Lincoln who said that "you cannot have the right to do what is wrong," and it was Theodore Roosevelt who said that "no man is justified in doing evil on the ground of expediency." So no, the ends do not justify the means.

ABOUT JANUARY 6: "...CASTING ABOUT TO PRESERVE THEIR REPUTATIONS..."

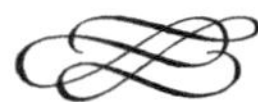

The conversations and arguments about voting in our Country reached a fever pitch on January 6, 2021, with a mob, bent on insurrection, invading and trashing our US Capitol. Their actions led to deaths and the second impeachment of then-president Trump. Our own Wisconsin elected federal officials, Sen. Johnson and Rep. Tiffany, were also on public record in support of challenging the honesty and fairness of the presidential election, the lynchpin words that helped precipitate the mob activities.

Voting is both a privilege and a right. It has not always been so. That is why this month and year may be especially important to highlight the birthday of one of the most remarkable persons in our history who gave her life in pursuit of voting rights for all, especially Black Americans and women. Susan B. Anthony Day is an annual celebration on February 15th to mark the birthday of this prominent civil rights leader and a major leader of the woman's suffrage movement in the United States. In Wisconsin, as in several states, it is a legal observance. Wisconsin was the first state to enact February 15 as a state holiday, doing so on April 15, 1976. As is most often the case with significant social change, it would take several generations after her death in 1906 for her birthday to be commemorated as a holiday.

Susan B. Anthony was born in a Quaker family on February 15, 1820. Her family was very committed to social equality, and, from them, she developed a sense of justice and the tenacity to pursue her moral convictions. She said that "cautious, careful people, always casting about to preserve their reputations... can never effect a reform." In 1851 she met Elizabeth Cady Stanton and together they would go on to join the woman's rights movement in 1852. The same year, Susan B. Anthony also became an agent for the American Anti-Slavery Society.

Despite vigorous opposition, abuse, and arrest, she continued until her death, on March 13, 1906, to travel the country in support of women's suffrage and the abolition of slavery. She had learned to read by the age of three and became a teacher where she earned $2.50 a week while male teachers earned $10.00 a week. In 1872 she was convicted and jailed for voting and was also fined $100. She had a strong distrust of church leaders in her day, saying that "I always distrust people who know so much about what God wants them to do to their fellows." On a brighter note, she was the first female in U.S. history to be placed on a circulating coin.

Why do we need social reformers like Susan B. Anthony? Because they and their work have proven to be essential to giving marginalized groups opportunities that were previously denied to them; to have a say in the society in which they lived; and to receive the basic human rights they needed to function as a part of their society. It is the work of social reformers that have given many, if not most, of us a sense of belonging and a sense of importance to the communities in which we live.

I know. There are still some groups that benefit more than others. There are still those who see most social change as a threat to cultural norms. But as Susan B. Anthony well demonstrated, social reforms can transform the world we live in and allow people with different backgrounds and diverse views to live in peace and work together toward the common good. Voting rights for all citizens is one of those reforms. Exercising it freely, fairly, and without fraud allowed again for a peaceful transfer of power. Thank you, Susan B. Anthony.

AN IRATE, TIRELESS MINORITY...

Sometimes I just sit and sigh. Then I often seek out something to read from our founders or a noted historical figure. This quote from one of our founders, Samuel Adams (yes, the beer guy), reflected my thinking about our current state of affairs: "It does not take a majority to prevail ... but rather an irate, tireless minority, keen on setting brushfires of freedom in the minds of men." Very recently we have seen elected members of a state government expelled, a candidate for our highest public office extolling the virtues of the three most notorious autocratic leaders on the planet, and the profound disregard of people in leadership toward a huge majority in public opinion, choosing guns over innocent lives. While those are only a few examples, the public discourse increasingly includes concern about the rise of authoritarianism.

Beginning in the nineteenth century, authoritarianism came to be described as the view which promoted a hierarchical leadership where one person, or one group, is dominant and governs the rest of us in a manner that compels voluntary obedience without question. Authority is demonstrated when others will do something simply on command. The word *authority* comes from the Latin *auctoritas*, which means "a kind of intangible social authority tied to reputation and status."

Assenting to authority is a part of all of our lives. Having authoritarian leaders is of a different scale. Almost seventy-five years ago, Theodor W. Adorno and his colleagues studied authoritarianism in America. Entitled "The Authoritarian Personality," they admitted that their study had to recognize "the potential (for desiring authoritarianism) existing in the character of the people." They identified two different types of authoritarianism. The first they called "authoritarian submission" in which some people think our country is in desperate need of a mighty, strong, and dominant leader. The second type they called "authoritarian aggression." These are people who think we need a leader who will destroy and eliminate the things perceived as ruining our country.

A review of this historic book reminds one that authoritarianism in America has a long and dark history. In the 1930s and '40s, numerous far-right groups exerted extremist pressures in our government until they were exposed as the "Nazi Underworld of America." In the 1950s, there were the witch hunts known as McCarthyism, which focused on treason and "subversives" in our federal government. Beginning in the 1970s and continuing to this day, the fundamentalistic religious right increasingly blended with politics to promote and force minority ideas upon the majority. Seventy years of studies have shown that those who tend to be very religious often move toward authoritarianism, with fundamentalists having the strongest association with authoritarian ideas. Those ideas include submission to authority and conventionality, respect for social order, and an intolerance for outside groups. In other words, what the Adorno study exposed was the social and psychological context in which an authoritarian leader or group could rise. It is a part of our past, it is a part of our present.

Finally, the study underscores how political "gaslighting" is favored by authoritarians. The term comes from the 1930s play "Gas Light" in which a manipulative husband tries to fool his wife by meddling with her perception of reality. He dims the gaslights and pretends it's only she who thinks they are flickering as the rooms grow darker. Like authoritarians, he exerts power and control by creating doubts about what is real and what isn't.

Yet it is in ordinary Americans like most of us that Adorno s study finds its remedy. Authoritarianism can be cleansed through a widespread and robust willingness to reject it, and to replace it with demanding, sometimes precarious, and always hard labor-intensive efforts at maintaining and restoring a democracy. President Lincoln said it best: "We the people are the rightful masters of both Congress and the courts, not to overthrow the Constitution but to overthrow the men who pervert the Constitution." In other words, vote 'em out!

GOVERNMENT FOR THE FEW,
PAID FOR BY THE MANY

From 1913–21, Woodrow Wilson was our president. He was the only president we have ever had who earned the Ph.D. degree. He also received the Nobel Peace prize and implemented many of the benefits that we enjoy to this day. It is this quote from him that has reinvigorated my belief in a democracy: "I believe in democracy because it releases the energies of every human being." It is that perspective that energizes our desires to promote and sustain our democracy. What Wilson meant by his statement was that we cannot leave our destiny to politicians, elites, and experts; either we take democracy into our own hands, or others will take democracy from us.

Across the country, our eighteenth-century political system is failing to deal with basic realities. Despite Thomas Jefferson's counsel that we would need a revolution every 25 years to best serve new generations, our structure, practically deified for 247 years, has essentially stayed the same while science and technology have advanced. In one way or another, this is the oldest story in America. The storyline remains the same. It is a continuing struggle to determine whether "We, the People" is a political reality embodied in the "one nation, indivisible" proclamation, or just a charade making it possible for the powerful and privileged to sustain their own way of life at the expense of others.

We seem to be just biding our time, trying to decide what kind of country we want to be. While marking time as this is happening, powerful interests sowing fear-based discontent are making off with the loot. Beginning a half of a century ago, a small group of political, corporate, and religious fundamentalists began the process of remaking politics and made grievance-based inequality their goal. They launched what became a crusade to dissemble and dismember the political institutions, the legal and statutory rules we had agreed to share, and the intellectual and cultural frameworks that have held private power. And they, later aided by the Citizens United Supreme Court ruling (2010), had the money to back up their ambition.

The sad and sometimes overwhelming truth is we cannot build a reasonably united political society across the immense divides that define our country today. To bridge that divide and make society more whole will require sharing the benefits of freedom and prosperity with the many who are defined as the least among us. When powerful and self-serving interests shower our elected representatives in Washington, and in virtually every state, with millions in campaign contributions, they often get what they want. But it is ordinary citizens and smaller businesses that pay the price, and most of us never see it coming. That is what happens if we don't contribute to their campaigns or spend generously on lobbying. And so we pick up a disproportionate share of America's tax bill. We pay taxes that they have been excused from paying. We abide by laws while others are granted immunity from them. We pay debts that we incur while others do not. We run our businesses by one set of rules, while there is another set for our larger competitors. In contrast, the fortunate few who contribute to the right politicians and hire the right lobbyists enjoy all the benefits of their special status. If they want to kill legislation that is intended for the public good, it gets killed. America now has "government for the few at the expense of the many." Thomas Jefferson also said that "the care of human life and happiness, and not their destruction, is the first and only object of good government." That sounds like a good place to refocus our efforts.

A REFORMATION THOUGHT
BEFORE ANY ELECTION

Since the beginning of the Protestant Reformation in 1517, over five hundred years have passed. Many Christian churches, particularly Lutheran, celebrated the five-hundredth anniversary of that historical Reformation. Thinking about the many religious concerns that gave rise to the Reformation, I recently found my thoughts focusing on one of Martin Luther's concerns, even though it was likely a secondary concern. That concern had to do with the relative relationship between our emotions and our intellect.

Most election cycles, primarily on the presidential level, demonstrate the contrast between emotions and intellect in stark relief. Both presidential candidates, to greater or lesser degree, have generated strong feelings (emotions) of like or dislike, depending upon which political party is yours. Often these feelings seem mostly unaffected by the use of one's intellect or thought. So Martin Luther provides a cautionary tale about the uses of these important and necessary human attributes.

In short, if either our emotions or our intellect becomes the "master" of the other, the likelihood of a balanced understanding decreases. Nonetheless, whether it is in love or politics or religion, it is most often the fickleness of feelings, relatively unaffected by intellect or thought, that seems to get us into trouble.

So as you approach any election, most of which seem to be part of an endless election process, perhaps the words of Pearl Buck (American writer, 1892-1973) have some merit: "You cannot make yourself feel something you do not feel, but you can make yourself do right in spite of your feelings." Keep that thought in mind as you enter the voting booth on any election day.

SECTION III

COMMON SENSE THINKING ABOUT RELIGION

re·li·gion ri-ˈli-jən : a personal set or institutionalized system of religious attitudes, beliefs, and practices: the service and worship of God or the supernatural: commitment or devotion to religious faith or observance: a cause, principle, or system of beliefs held to with ardor and faith.

A COMMON BASE

I confess. I am one of those silent/mature generation members, joined by some of the earlier baby boomers, who every Friday for many months has stood on a street to protest. The word *protest*, by the way, is a positive word. It is made up of two Latin words, *pro* and *testamentum*. It means we stand FOR something, for some belief or value or promise or covenant. The people who drive by and respond (many just ignore us) don't always stand for what we stand for, and they let us know that with a thumb down or a finger up or a shouted phrase that, even at my advanced age, embarrasses me.

The times we are living in are troubling. Here as elsewhere, intolerance, hatred, bigotry, and racism have been seething out of the shadows and manifesting in ways not seen for decades. We have seen the increased activity and visibility of neo-Nazis, white supremacists, anti-Muslim activists, and the Ku Klux Klan. Because of that and for other reasons, I protest. I stand for the increase of love and peace. Why?

Because one of the core principles or values that runs uniformly through the world's major religious teachings — at least as expressed by Jehovah, Jesus, Mohammed, Buddha, Krishna, Sankara, Confucius, and others—is the concept of loving our neighbors, conquering fear with love. It is the belief that behaviors based upon faith and prayer and meditation can provide us with the strength that allows love for our fellow humans to become an abiding part of our lives. Love is a unifying force. A second core principle is the unifying power of seeking peace. When people live in the awareness that there is a close kinship between all individuals and nations, peace is the natural result.

On the other hand, hate groups are energized and empowered by sowing terror and fear. Their purpose is to divide us against one another as a means of leading us to scapegoat and hate those who are different from us. Religious groups and minorities are particularly targeted by such ideological extremists here in the USA and else-where. This behavior, which is the antithesis of seeking love and peace, can have tragic consequences for unmeasured numbers of people.

I expect that the majority of you reading this stand together with all people of good will, religious and non-religious, in stating categor-ically your abhorrence and rejection of any rhetoric or action that incites one group of people to vilify and diminish another group for any reason. I expect that same majority would categorically reject any expressions of hatred, racism, intolerance, and bigotry, even towards those who are full of hate themselves. The foundational religious concepts of love and peace are acted out by committing ourselves to welcoming all into our communities and to promoting inclusivity as a community norm.

RESETTING OUR MORAL COMPASS

My spouse and I like to eat breakfast at local restaurants. One of our favorite places is a local bar/restaurant combination where the price is right, the food is good, the bartender/waiter and cook are favorite people, and the customers offer personal insights (often vehemently) on all the controverted issues of the day. On a recent visit, a discussion at the bar seemed to produce more heat than light, leading the bartender/waiter to say, as he delivered our breakfast, "We just need to return to our moral compass." I agreed, but then wondered exactly what we mean by wanting to follow a "moral compass." Maybe we can just agree that by placing the word *moral* in front of *compass*, we are speaking about the mental processes we use that direct our attitudes and behaviors in life. Of course, we must admit that one person's moral compass might not point in the same direction as another person's. Nonetheless, 247 years of living together in the community we call the USA has produced certain shared values under law and experience that reflect our moral compass. These primary values include respect, tolerance, honesty, and integrity.

Respect means to value self and others. It is living with dignity and showing dignity toward others. Being closed-minded, critical, and maintaining a superior attitude with regard to one's values is destructive of our relationships with others.

Tolerance means that we are willing to put up with something we consider either wrong or displeasing, but not so much that we feel compelled to constrain it. It does not mean that we must approve of something as good when we consider it otherwise. Tolerance, however, is essential in an imperfect world. Why? Because we all have family members, friends, and acquaintances who are people we like but, as with every human, who can also be annoying or exhibit undesirable traits. Without tolerance, we would be involved in power struggles or fruitless battles to make each person perfect according to our own standards. Being tolerant means that we accept less desirable aspects in people (using our personal definitions) in order to attain higher values such as respect, kindness, harmony, friendship, mercy, etc.

Honesty means more than not lying, as important as that is. It also means not doing things that break the law or are considered morally wrong. Honesty is about speaking and acting truthfully. It includes not hiding the truth, not breaking rules to gain an advantage, not taking something that isn't yours, and not doing any other action that you would hide because it is against what you consider morally or legally right. Without a cultural agreement on the importance of truth-telling, and a cultural demonstration of honesty in daily living, a culture quickly slips into prejudice, bigotry, xenophobia, and division.

Integrity is about doing the right thing even when it's not acknowledged by others, or convenient for you. An individual with integrity possesses the antidote to self-interest. Living with integrity is behaving honestly and practicing ethical behavior in your interactions. It avoids political and self-serving behavior. It is courageously standing up for what you believe in. It is being a role model for living your values.

If the next generations are going to be successful in navigating the many and diverse complexities that lie ahead and do so in a manner that results in richer, deeper, and more meaningful lives, following these values will again help us to unite in vision and purpose.

A DIVINE IDEA

Please allow me to set the context. As far as historians, archeologists, and anthropologists can determine, virtually all known societies, past and present, have some form of a belief in a superior or supreme being or beings. While there are always people in some of the cultures who do not share such a belief, five of the major religions account for almost 75 percent of religious adherents. All these major religions have subdivided themselves into numerous subgroups. Christianity, as one example, has subdivided itself into thirty-four thousand separate groups, one of which is Lutheranism which has subdivided itself into twenty-five distinct groups just in the USA. Given that context, it seems almost incredible that a majority of religious adherents would agree on anything. Nonetheless, as we again approach Earth Day (this is the 53rd year this day is celebrated), a quick review of what the five major religions believe about the relationship between a divine presence and the planet we all share might be informative. It surely comes as a surprise!

Christians generally believe that the earth and all forms of life on it are gifts from God, given us to share and develop not to dominate and exploit. The material resources of the earth and the beauties of nature are to be enjoyed and celebrated as well as consumed. Given that perspective, we nonetheless have the responsibility to create a lifestyle balance between consumption and conservation. We are called by God to consider the welfare of future generations in our plans for and uses of the earth's resources. We are expected to pass on the planet earth in at least the same and, hopefully, better condition than we received it.

Muslims believe in *Tawhid* or the Unity of God. *Allah* is Unity, which is reflected in the unity of humankind, and in the unity of humans and nature. We are God's trustees and are responsible for maintaining the unity of God's creation, the integrity of the earth, its flora and fauna, and its wildlife and natural environment. Unity cannot be achieved by setting one need against another or letting one end predominate over another; it is maintained by balance and harmony. Muslims believe that people are expected to maintain balance and harmony in the whole of creation around us.

Hinduism is very concerned with the relationship between humanity and the environment. Karma teaches that resources in the world become scarce because people use them for their own ends. People should use the world unselfishly in order to maintain the natural balance and to repay God for the gifts God has given.

Buddhists believe that the reality of the interconnectedness of human beings, society, and nature will reveal itself more and more to us as we gradually cease to be possessed by anxiety, fear, and the dispersion of the mind. Among the three—human beings, society, and nature—it is us who begin to effect change. But in order to effect change, we must seek the kind of lifestyle that is free from the destruction of one's humanness. Efforts to change the environment and to change oneself are both necessary. But we know how difficult it is to change the environment if individuals themselves are not in a state of equilibrium.

Judaism defines the relationship between God and the land as continuous and longer lasting than any relationship we may have with it. Thus, in Leviticus, God informs people that no land can be sold forever, for "the land is Mine – you are but strangers resident with Me." Later Rabbinic commentaries continued this theme: "God acquired possession of the world and apportioned it to humanity, but God always remains the Ruler of the world." God is, therefore, Creator of this world and created human beings in the firm understanding that they are never permanent residents on the earth – we continue to live on earth only by the grace of God.

Politicians may argue, scientists may disagree, and climate change deniers may still pontificate, but the major religions are all unified in their belief that the earth is God's and humans are the caretakers. A good reminder to ponder as we again celebrate Earth Day on April 22.

MAJORING IN MINORS?

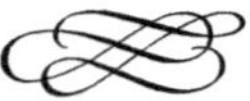

When I was a seminary student almost sixty years ago, a favorite professor reminded us that as pastors we should always work hard to make sure that we weren't majoring in minors. In other words, our priorities were to reflect those of the founder and object of our faith – Christian in my case. I honestly do not know how that advice is working out right now, even though 65 percent of us still admit to being Christians. Nonetheless, in our "Christian" nation, we have almost unchecked public lying, gross economic inequality, an uncaring attitude about the unmet health needs of millions, the refusal and abuse of immigrants seeking a more humane life, and the marginalization of many because of race, ethnicity, sexuality, and social class. Addressing and seeking change in all those behaviors were "majors" in the life and work of our founder.

What resurfaced my conscience and consciousness was a call from a former student, now well matured, who had just interviewed for a pastoral position at a regional area church. He said he blew it at the end of the interview when one member of the search committee asked, "Reverend, would you please tell us how you feel about abortion and homosexuality." He answered by saying, "Why are you asking me about abortion? The word is not even in the Judeo-Christian

Scriptures or the Qur'an. The Prophets didn't talk about it, Jesus never mentioned it, and the Apostles never spoke of it. And homosexuality? Jesus never said a word about it. Do you have a problem with homosexuals at this church? Are they lying or stealing money from the poor or being inhospitable to strangers? Why do you want to know how I feel about those two things? Why don't you want to know how I feel about caring for the poor, and the disenfranchised, and the sick and non-sick without health insurance, and the maltreated and mistreated immigrants and their children locked away in cells, and the racial and ethnic minorities suffering from generations of discrimination? Why don't you ask me a question that matters to the well-being of this community?"

The pastor did not receive the offer to serve at that parish. The word *Christian* means "little Christ." It means that when we wear that descriptor, we pledge our daily behavior to be in conformity with the words and actions of Christ. Maybe Gautam Buddha said it best when he said that "however many holy words you read, however many you speak, what good will they do you if you do not act upon them?" It seems like a good universal precept to apply as we seek always to major in majors. I know that some will disagree with the perspective related above, and some do not live a faith tradition that guides their behavior. Whatever the case, the advice to not major in minors speaks to those behaviors that reflect how we prioritize things that matter in our lives. Things like holding "these truths to be self-evident, that all men are created equal, that they are endowed by their Creator with certain unalienable Rights, that among these are Life, Liberty and the pursuit of Happiness."

SEPARATION OF CHURCH AND STATE

Our US Supreme Court, by majority decisions (5-4), handed down two rulings that in the eyes of some violated our Constitutional separation of powers, and, in the eyes of others, clarified it. This is a good moment to remind ourselves that those who persist in calling America a Christian nation founded on Judeo-Christian principles are operating with a deception and a myth that are unfortunately still being publicly shared with the American people. The founding fathers called instead for a secular state, where religion could be practiced in a voluntary way, and they insisted on the separation of church and state. The US Constitution says very clearly that "there shall be no established religion."

Historians tell us that during the Revolutionary period between 1750 and 1800, the influence of the Christian church and its beliefs was at its lowest ebb in the history of America. In fact, the few Christian ministers who spoke out between 1787 and 1789 denounced the proposed Constitution as godless, anti-Christian, Jewish, Islamic, deistic, pagan, and atheistic. It has been said that at that time in our history, only between six and eleven percent of the American people were actively involved in the Christian church. Surely, some of the founding fathers were Christians. Many of them, however, were not

Christians, at least in the conventional understanding of the word, and this included the most influential of those who drafted the Declaration of Independence and the Constitution.

Most of our country's founders were rationalists who operated with reason alone, and many of them were deists. Rationalists held that any claim to supernatural revelation was false. John Adams even felt that organized religion was harmful. Many of the founders who were deists, including Washington, Adams, Jefferson, and Franklin among many others, believed that the course of nature gave evidence to the existence of God, but they felt that formal religion was unnecessary.

With regard to the specific history about the separation of church and state, Jefferson, in his 1802 letter to some Connecticut Baptists, said,

Believing with you that religion is a matter which lies solely between Man & his God, that he owes account to none other for his faith or his worship, that the legitimate powers of government reach actions only, & not opinions, I contemplate with sovereign reverence that act of the whole American people which declared that their legislature should "make no law respecting an establishment of religion, or prohibiting the free exercise thereof," thus building a wall of separation between Church & State.

As recently as 1984, in a speech to a Jewish community in California, Ronald Reagan said,

We in the United States, above all, must remember that lesson, for we were founded as a nation of openness to people of all beliefs. And so we must remain. Our very unity has been strengthened by our pluralism. We establish no religion in this country, we command no worship, we mandate no belief, nor will we ever. Church and state are, and must remain, separate. All are free to believe or not believe, all are free to practice a faith or not, and those who believe are free, and should be free, to speak of and act on their belief.

As you decide for yourself about the advisability of these recent court decisions, it is good to close with the reminder that it was the United States Treaty of Tripoli, Article 11 (negotiated during Washington's administration, unanimously ratified by the US Senate, and then signed by President Adams in 1797) that said "[T]he government of the United States of America is not in any sense founded on the Christian Religion." This statement in no way denigrates the role of religion in the formation of American history. However, the record must be made clear: the crucial period in the formation of the American republic (1750-1800) was marked by rationalism, which is reflected in our founding documents. No latter-day revisionism by the religious or political right will change that fact.

HALLOWEEN: RELIGIOUS AND SECULAR

This is how it began. It was called Samhain, a Celtic holiday celebrated two thousand years ago. It signified the end of the Celtic calendar year, the beginning of a cold and dark winter, and a time when ghosts of the dead roamed the earth at night.

Then in the eighth century, Pope Gregory III moved All Saints Day, a day honoring all the saints who did not already have their own day, to November 1 from May 13. While the reason for this move is still debated, the predominant idea is that Samhain was gaining in popularity at that time, and this was the pope's way of "Christianizing" a holiday considered to be pagan. As a result, the day before All Saints Day, All Hallows Eve (eventually shortened to Halloween), was the new "Christian" version of Samhain.

It was in the early nineteenth century that Halloween came to America, due primarily to Irish immigrants who settled here during the potato famine in Ireland. Along with them came their Halloween traditions of trick-or-treating and dressing up in costumes. Just as the original celebration of Samhain had to do with ghosts and the dead, today's most popular costumes still involve ghosts, witches, vampires, and the devil. Such costuming is derived from the Celtic origins of Halloween, but less so from the Christianized version of it. As such, some religions discourage or prohibit participation in Halloween. The decision to celebrate or not to celebrate is one of debate in these religious communities, especially among young families. Churches often put on fall or harvest festivals to give families an alternative to Halloween.

Based upon participation numbers, most Americans are either unaware of or ignore the religious concerns expressed by some. About 70 percent of Americans participate in Halloween activities; we are expected to spend $10.6 billion this year on Halloween festivities; and it is the fifth-largest drinking holiday. For many, it has evolved into a day of activities that also include carving jack-o-lanterns, festive gatherings, and eating treats.

What stands out, however, is the consumerist nature of the holiday and its related rituals. Our primary focus as we celebrate Halloween is to buy stuff. We do go out and get together and have fun, but none of that happens without first shopping and spending an estimated $10.1 billion. Halloween, like other holidays that have become consumerist (Christmas, New Year, Valentine's Day, Easter, Mother's and Father's Days), seems to be an occasion upon which we reaffirm the importance of consuming in order to fit in with the norms and expectations of society.

Perhaps that is not a bad idea. We are faced with a continuing barrage of terrible news about threats to our democracy, global climate change, violence and war, discrimination and injustice, and disease. Amid this, Halloween presents an alluring opportunity to take off our own identity, put on another, evade our cares and concerns, and exist as someone else for an evening or two. Happy Halloween!

THANKSGIVING A MYTH?

I was stunned several years ago when I read about the history of Thanksgiving on the Smithsonian's web page (Smithsonian.org). It reminded me of moving to North Carolina in the early 70s and taking our young girls to Carowinds, a theme park straddling the North and South Carolina borders. The featured movie that summer was about "The War Between the States." It was with a sense of disbelief that we heard nothing about slavery, but heard instead about the North's attempt to reduce or remove the South's ability to compete economically. The explanatory perspective was the opposite of what we had learned and, in this case, was historically inaccurate.

It was the same kind of jarring alternative reality, written by exemplary historians, that challenged my thoughts about Thanksgiving. I had learned that the Indians were friendly (no tribe was ever mentioned) and that they welcomed the Pilgrims to America, taught them how to live in this new location, sat down to a dinner with them, and then mostly disappeared, leaving us to create this new nation.

Now we know that history didn't begin for Native Americans when the Europeans arrived, because they had already been in the Americas for least twelve thousand years and maybe longer. In addition, the arrival of the *Mayflower* was not their first contact with Europeans. By the time the Pilgrims arrived, at least two or more members of the local Wampanoag tribe spoke English, had already been to Europe and back, and knew the organizers of the Pilgrims' venture. They also owned property, not private property but community property, knowing where their people's land started and where it ended. In other words, when Europeans came to the Americas and bought land from the Wampanoags, they assumed the English were buying into the Wampanoag country, not buying the Wampanoag country out from under their feet.

That is just the beginning of a widely available sordid history about our Native American predecessors. Nonetheless, in 1863, Abraham Lincoln declared a national Thanksgiving holiday during the Civil War to foster unity. While we cannot forget our past, working toward national unity can help us to reclaim some national honor. We can begin by remembering that Thanksgiving is the only national holiday that asks us, individually and personally, to express gratitude. The other holidays ask us to celebrate a birth, a hero, or a sacrificial human experience. It is Thanksgiving that asks us to look inward and to consider, at the very least, an unselfish gratefulness for the many blessings that are unique to each of us in our lives.

The culture in which we live is usually focused outward. We like debate (too often becoming disputes or debacles), and our public conversations are often argumentative. It is Thanksgiving that serves as a counterbalance. It is a day which, in spite of different values, traditions, or perspectives, calls us to suspend the daily and often noisy disagreeableness for the sake of this internal moment. While we do not often celebrate this day with those with whom we disagree, we still know and affirm that it is also celebrated by those with whom we disagree. As such, it becomes a mark of our common humanness.

So yes, the other holidays each have their own unique qualities, but I often think it is Thanksgiving's uniqueness that best offers what we all need. It offers all 333 million of us, without regard for belief or background, an opportunity to recognize or remember not just what we are thankful for, but also whom we can be thankful to. Cicero said, "A thankful heart is not only the greatest virtue, but the parent of all other virtues." Happy Thanksgiving!

JUST WONDERING?

Do you ever wonder how all the commotion surrounding Christmas has come to this point? It is the holiday celebrated by the most Americans, and also the holiday around which people spend more money than any other. There are other religious holidays that occur near in the calendar year to Christmas, and we surely acknowledge their importance also in this season. Nonetheless, Christmas in our culture takes center stage at this time of the year.

Where does the word *Christmas* come from, and when did it originate? Even though it is now a highly secularized national holiday, most of us likely assume that *Christmas* comes from the word *Christ*. The whole idea of Christmas is, after all, to celebrate the birth of Jesus. The history, in summary, is this: in AD 1038 the term *Cristes Maesse* (Christ's Mass) was first used, followed by *Cristes Messe* in AD 1131. The word *Christ* (originally *Crist*) comes from the Greek word *Christos* which is a translation of the Hebrew word for Messiah (anointed one). The word *maesse* comes from the Latin *missa* meaning the liturgical Mass of the Eucharist.

The earliest Christians did not celebrate the birth of Christ, believing that it was a pagan (nonbeliever) practice to celebrate birthdays. Rather, Easter and Pentecost were the main celebrations until the middle of the fourth century, when Christmas and Epiphany were added. At about that same time, December 25 was identified as the Nativity Feast Day and the first "Nativity Mass" was celebrated. Finally, the Nativity Mass became the Christ's Mass (Christmas) by the eleventh century.

So much for background. Of all the holidays we celebrate, it is Christmas that brings forth the deepest and most hopeful feelings about peace. It just seems that a paradigm or template for peace in the world could somehow be found in the celebratory elements at this time of the year. Unfortunately, given the current political sniping and self-interest in our own country, and the alienation of our allies and others throughout the world, peace seems far away and increasingly unlikely. Hatred and prejudice and inequality, which seemed to be diminishing in recent decades, have increasingly reared their ugly heads.

Even so, we live in hope and celebrate with joy. To do otherwise would show that we have lost the belief that we can effect much-needed, positive change in our world. Being patient and persevering, in spite of seemingly stagnant change, are two essential attributes as we seek a more tolerant and peaceful world. Sometimes it can seem very hard to carry on as our efforts may seem fruitless, but we must keep trying to continue making positive changes which are the signet of our human family. And why? Because that is the message of the little baby in Bethlehem's manger; he did not come among us to divide us into tribes at war with one another, and he never demonstrated or approved of the use of anger to separate us one from another.

As we join together with family and friends in our homes during these holiday days, and in our churches, synagogues, and mosques, may we feel the sense of joy and hope that provides and sustains inner peace and awe. And may that sense of hope radiate beyond us to others so that hearts with similar hopes may connect and increase. In that way, we may accelerate the movement toward a kinder, more tolerant, and gentler world. And, of course, if we can keep that hope alive for more than just a day or two, we may even capture and keep the essence of this holiday to revisit again and again when the holiday season is completed. In doing that, change will come. Have a hopeful, joyful, and merry Christmas!

"WE'RE HERE FOR SOMETHING ELSE BESIDES OURSELVES."

The Peabody and Emmy Award-winning author and journalist, Eric Sevareid (1912-1992) said that "Christmas is a necessity. There has to be at least one day of the year to remind us that we're here for something else besides ourselves." For example, here is a news story about a very well-known man who had the opportunity to read his own obituary. His brother had died, but the newspaper mistakenly identified the death of the wrong brother. As he read the obituary, he was aghast that he was being referred to as the "dynamite king." This happened to Alfred Nobel, identified in the obituary as someone who got very rich from the manufacturing of a weapon of mass destruction. That definition was hurtful to him because when he invented dynamite, he thought it was going to be used as an instrument of peace and that no one would want to use such deadly power as a means of injuring others. Yet, nothing in his obituary talked of his many efforts to break down barriers that separated people from one another ... it only spoke about him as a merchant of death.

His response was in the form of a resolution, codified in his last will and testament, to set aside a huge fund that resulted in the Nobel Peace Prize, which would be given to those who have accomplished the most for world peace. The last Nobel Peace Prize (2022) was awarded to human rights advocate Ales Bialiatski from Belarus, the Russian human rights organization Memorial, and the Ukrainian human rights organization Center for Civil Liberties. The Norwegian Nobel Committee wrote that they were chosen "to honour three outstanding champions of human rights, democracy and peaceful co-existence in the neighbour countries Belarus, Russia and Ukraine. Through their consistent efforts in favour of humanist values, anti-militarism and principles of law, this year's laureates have revitalized and honoured Alfred Nobel's vision of peace and fraternity between nations – a vision most needed in the world today." The award ceremony is on December 10, to mark the day in 1896 that Alfred Nobel died.

What does that have to do with real life as we are closing out an often conflicted old year, and are close to entering a new year? Typically, cartoons depict the New Year as a baby, full of possibilities and innocence. We usually hope that with a new year we can leave the negative and hurtful baggage behind us, and stretch toward a brighter future. But at the same time, we cannot help but see the darkness in society and politics: the bickering between the political parties that is based upon self and party priorities above the needs of the common good and leads to cynicism; the violation of democratic principles to retain political power; the extreme disparity in the distribution of wealth and power; and the healthcare system that leaves many millions unprotected and overcharges most of the rest of us, as a few examples.

We wonder what this coming year (2024) will hold for us? Will it be the year that we get our act together and remember that "we're here for something else besides ourselves"? Will it be the year that the politicians clean up the corruption? Will it be the year that science finds a breakthrough for cancer or any of the other diseases that threaten us? We do not know what 2024 holds for us. Likely, we will experience grace and love along with the pain and frustration. We will see the darkness in its full fury. We will also see shafts of light that burst through the darkness. I hope we can hold on to those shafts of light this holiday season with courage, because we know that as light shines in the darkness, and each of us shares grace and healing in our darkened world, the light of hope and change will follow. After all, "we're here for something else besides ourselves." A blessed holiday season to all!

A HOPEFUL CHRISTMAS WISH

We are in the season where the words peace, love, joy, and hope prevail in the public arena. It is, therefore, heartbreaking to see people in our community, and throughout the USA, being separated from one another over issues about the 2020 election, about CDC recommendations, about what is taught in our schools, and about religious beliefs. There has been and continues to be debate, both embarrassing and sometimes violent, about such issues. Socrates was insightful when he said that "when the debate is lost, slander becomes the tool of the loser."

In a recent article in The Atlantic, I found myself identifying with the two-thirds of Americans who they called the "exhausted majority." We are the folks who "share a sense of fatigue with our polarized national conversation, a willingness to be flexible in their political viewpoints, and a lack of voice in the national conversation." So why do we let the losing minority have such a disproportionate "voice in the national conversation?" Or better yet, a prior question – why do some people have such a difficult time losing? Didn't our parents teach us to be "good losers"?

Part of the answer goes back to a 1950's study by the preeminent psychologist, Leon Festinger, titled *When Prophecy Fails.* He had studied a cult named The Seekers who believed an apocalypse would occur on a certain date. When it did not, they didn't question their beliefs but came up with alternative explanations. To explain this strengthened belief in a coming apocalypse in the face of undeniable opposite evidence, Festinger proposed cognitive dissonance as an explanation.

Cognitive dissonance happens when we encounter something that challenges our beliefs, attitudes, or normal behaviors. It makes us uncomfortable because it flies in the face of what we think or want to be true. It can lead some of us to the point where we are unable to accept certain outcomes even in the face of overwhelming diametrically opposed evidence.

More recently, the interaction between cognitive dissonance and the concept of grandiose narcissism has also been studied. While the concept of narcissism dates to ancient Greek times, a grandiose narcissistic individual is currently defined as being competitive, dominant, has an inflated positive self-image regarding one's own skills, abilities, and attributes, and an inflated self-worth. When presented with contrary evidence, such as defeat or failure, the grandiose narcissist usually experiences cognitive dissonance. In attempting to reduce the distress caused by this dissonance, the grandiose narcissist redirects and places the blame on someone or something else. This strategy of reducing dissonance allows the grandiose narcissists' self-image to stay intact. To admit being wrong as well as to apologize for a mistake or bad behavior would severely damage their self-image – something they could not allow.

We yearn for peace, love, joy, and hope especially in this season. The billionaire businessman, Thomas Peterffy, offers encouragement to those who find losing difficult to manage. He says that "self-discipline is what separates the winners and the losers." Hopefully, those who are poor losers will use this season of peace, love, and hope to redevelop the self-discipline it takes to review, reflect, and hopefully revise their thoughts, beliefs, and behaviors. Why? Because as the American Poet, Carl Sandburg, said: "To be a good loser is to learn how to win."

THOUGHTS ABOUT FLAG WAVING
ON ENTERING A NEW YEAR

We are about to close out a year of more flag waving than I can remember within the context of my life. We all love the flags, the rah-rah's, the warm feelings, the deep respect, and the gratitude we have for the gift of our country. But this past year the flag waving seemed to become divisive rather than unifying. I think it may be that in the minds of some, patriotism and chauvinism have become confused. The word *chauvinism* comes from Nicholas Chauvin, a soldier in Napoleon's army who was blindly loyal to Napoleon. Chauvinism is zealous and aggressive patriotism, a conviction that we are better because we are chosen. It expresses itself in excessive enthusiasm for military glory and holds no room for difference of opinion. It believes that "God is on our side" and puts blind, uncritical faith in one's leader or leaders. Please, please, as we enter another year, consider the following perspectives, and do your own research to test them for veracity:

- Patriotism is not to be based on the mistaken premise that America was founded as a Christian nation. Our historical documents reflect the spirits of our founders as people who were fearful of religious interference in the rule of law.

Those who think otherwise reflect the spirit of Cotton Mather and later American thinkers who believed that Americans are a chosen people with a special destiny. According to historical facts, the founders were rationalists and deists.

- Patriotism holds America to the ideals on which it was founded. Our founding documents charge our government with the responsibility to serve the common good. They emphasize that all people are created equal and have the right to life, liberty, justice, and the pursuit of happiness. There is also the constitutional insistence on the separation of church and state. Although the vision of America enshrined in our founding documents is consistent with the Christian biblical vision of peace and wholeness, it does not advocate a theocracy (a country ruled by God, or the people who say they speak for God) in America.

- Patriotism is based on compassion, not hatred. Compassion is the foundation on which we build the just society envisioned by our founders. At the end of 2023, our country remains divided on many issues, including the gross division between the haves and the have-nots. True patriots will strive to pay the price so that the underclasses and all those who are denied access to the American dream of liberty and justice for all will share in it.

- Patriotism affirms the unity in our diversity. One of our greatest gifts is that diverse peoples are striving to live together in a reconciled way, all adding different gifts to the strengthening of our country. We all share in a common underlying humanity and underlying dream. Sadly, this vision of a diverse yet unified America is not now reflected in reality. One measure of patriotism is a commitment to support the inclusion of all Americans in the promise of the American dream.

- Finally, an authentic patriot has the courage to call our leaders to accountability. Patriotism keeps the focus on our historical vision. When that vision is defiled, patriots are willing to stand in opposition to policies that are unjust, do not reflect the high ideals on which this country was founded, and are destructive of the common good. Patriots address the devastating realities of our times by such actions as becoming informed about the founding vision of our country, working to elect wise and compassionate leaders, and being prepared to sacrifice so that others might share in America's promise.

I hope the year 2024 will find both an increasing majority demonstrating historic patriotism and a continually decreasing chauvinistic minority.

IN THIS NEW YEAR, I STILL FIND IT DIFFICULT TO ADMIT BEING A CHRISTIAN

It is the first few days of a new year, and I must finally admit that the last few years have made it increasingly burdensome for me to admit being a Christian. It is in no way related to my relationship with Jesus or the Christian Gospel. It is specifically related to my increasing distress with the toxic and destructive brand of Christianity that continues to use its influence to assert and defend nationalism, to tolerate and promote white supremacy, to advance and expand false and baseless conspiracy theories, and to thereby cede traditional Christian convictions in exchange for political power. Christians are no longer expressing differences in theological opinions but seem instead to be following different gods.

How does this happen? It was Voltaire who said that "in the beginning God created man in His own image, and man has been trying to repay the favor ever since." In other words, if God made us like God, our religions have gone out of their way to make God look like us. In sociology, we define this as *totemism* (from a North American Ojibwe word), meaning humans who are said to have a mystical relationship with a spiritual being. In practice, it means that our strongly held opinions rarely differ from what we think is God's word on the matter. As Anne Lamott once said, "You can safely assume you've created God in your image when it turns out God hates all the same people you do."

Again, how does this happen? We make up a Jesus that fits ourselves because this invented character makes so very few actual demands of us. He makes us happy without challenging us, and doesn't suggest that we do something about the troubled circumstances of the world. Of course, calling us to address the real plight of the world is what the real Jesus had an uncomfortable habit of doing. Still, we want to subdue and harness who Jesus was, even as His life and ministry will not allow it. Cultural and social barriers were shattered by Him. We also tend to join faith communities that agree with our preferred version of Jesus. In doing so, we become surrounded with people of like mind who rarely challenge our priorities, values, or beliefs, and any valid criticism is interpreted to be an attack on God.

While I fight being a cynic about the future of Christianity, I do affirm that the behaviors I have described are normal, in part, because that is how people organize themselves within society. It is not just Christians or religious people who do this, because none of us, including me, are untouched by this influence. At the same time, it also helps to explain why many of us feel so spiritually and politically homeless. This may be especially true for a generation of young people who are far more concerned about making a difference in the world than preserving the current status quo, including a mythical version of America that only exists in the minds of those unschooled in history. Those who have left the Christian church didn't leave because their atheist professors perverted their thinking, but because they saw very public parts of the Christian church more interested in defending a political party than in loving and caring for their neighbors.

In this new year, I recognize that this critique does not define all Christians. For many self-identified evangelical Christians, however, I recommend getting to work reconstructing something better. A good beginning point might be to remember that the word *evangel* (from the Latin *evangelium* and the Greek *euangélion*) comes from the early words of Jesus to bring "good news" to the poor, the oppressed, the powerless, the immigrant. This new year provides us all an opportunity to see that the current story being told by God is that we are in the midst of breaking down barriers we erected out of our own misguided attempts to define God in our self-image, and replacing those barriers with the good news that brings hope and peace and joy to everyone.

AN EPIPHANY WISH: REASON AND REASONABLENESS

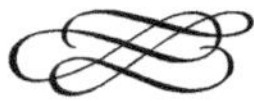

To many in the western world, Epiphany (January 6) brings the season of Christmas to a close. The word itself often refers to a moment when you become conscious of or feel that you better understand something of importance. The year 2023 is on the way to a conclusion, and the various histories of the events of last year are yet to be written. One thing still remains sure. For the first time in our 247-year history, a group of our fellow citizens invaded our national Capitol building with violent and destructive force in an attempt to deny a duly and fairly elected President his rightful ascension to leadership. It has been called an insurrection. According to the Cambridge Dictionary, the word means "an organized attempt by a group of people to defeat their government and take control of their country, usually by violence."

That event on January 6, 2021, Epiphany, continues to haunt our present and our future and calls us again to humble reflection and honest self-examination of our own individual values, beliefs, and hopes for our country and world as we enter 2024. Given that reality, my personal epiphany was clarified when I read this quote by Dr. Albert Einstein (1879-1955): "All of us who are concerned for peace and triumph of reason and justice must be keenly aware how small an influence reason and honest good will exert upon events in the political field." It seems to be a human frailty to be reticent to use our reason in a manner that promotes peace and goodwill among our fellow citizens. Specifically, why is it so difficult to be reasonable in our dealings with others, especially those with whom we disagree?

It is easier to expose our human frailties than to address them. The effort it takes to diminish our frailties often demands more change than we might be willing to accomplish. We know we have to be able to reason in order to be reasonable. Assuming that is the case, how do we define the ability to reason? The dictionary says that reason is "the power of the mind to think, understand, and form judgments by a process of logic." The definition is easy to read, but to accomplish it takes effort and time and contemplation and study.

I have not always been very good at fulfilling resolutions for change when a new year begins. Maybe an Epiphany resolution will hold more promise. I resolve, therefore, to work harder to use my reason to temper my feelings so that I can be more reasonable, especially toward those with whom I disagree. I hope you share the perspective that whatever effort and study it takes to reason and to be reasonable, it is worth it all in the hope of improving our track record in search of peace and good will.

BLESSED ARE THE FLEXIBLE...

As some of you know, in Christianity there are a set of teachings from Jesus (in the Gospels of Matthew and Luke) that begin with the phrase, "Blessed are ...." They are called the beatitudes and generally focus on a spirit of humility, love, mercy, and compassion. I heard the following beatitude stated recently and, even though it is *not* in the Christian Scriptures, I wish it had been!

"Blessed are the flexible, for they shall not be bent out of shape!" Over two thousand years ago, after experimenting with first a life of indulgence and then a life of asceticism, Buddha finally decided the "middle path" between the extremes was the best way to live a fulfilling life. Jesus also gave numerous examples of the need for flexibility in seeking a common good. Today, the behavioral sciences seem to be catching up with these ideas, as research on mental and social well-being is being pursued. The idea is not to strive blindly for more of everything that is perceived as "good" or "positive," but rather to use the entire range of emotions that we have at our disposal to move us towards the things that we value most. In short, it speaks of the ability to use the right emotional resources at the right times in order to create the kind of lives we want.

If this appeals to you, here is a brief summary of the areas of research to aid us as we seek to be "blessed" for our flexibility:

- *Acknowledgement:* Emotions such as pain, sadness, anger, and regret are all a part of life. Acknowledging and accepting negative emotions and experiences, rather than trying to control or eliminate them, is a healthier way to approach the complexities of human life. Acknowledging and accepting such emotions breaks the vicious cycle of having anxiety about the fact that you are having anxiety.
- *Inquisitiveness:* An inquisitive mindset allows you to observe your negative reactions without judgment and see what you can learn from them. Inquisitiveness engages your sense of logic and inhibits emotional "gut" reactions, allowing you to learn from these situations and identify intelligent next steps that lead you towards your goals.
- *Dedication:* Once your mind is freed from the exhausting struggle that comes from resisting or stressing about emotional states, it is easier to dedicate yourself to the right actions or behaviors that lead you towards the things that you value most.

So, if we find ourselves being inflexible because of negative thoughts and emotions, use the experience as an opportunity to stretch emotionally, to increase wisdom, and to grow in maturity. "Blessed are the flexible ...."

PATRIOTISM: WHOLESOME OR HARMFUL?

I t may be a good time to again reflect upon some thoughts based on continuing public conversations about "white nationalism" and "Christian nationalism," and the combination that is often used, namely, "white Christian nationalism." Merriam-Webster's definition of *nationalism* sets the stage for mischief: "Loyalty and devotion to a nation. A sense of national consciousness exalting one nation above all others and placing primary emphasis on promotion of its culture and interests as opposed to those of other nations or supranational groups." What is the difference between a patriotic devotion to our country that is wholesome and one that is harmful? That is one question. The second question is, "How do you know if you have changed from one type of devotion to the other?" I think we can agree that many millions of Americans, both religious and non-religious, have a deep love for our country. It is also a fairly common belief that our country has accomplished exceptional things that have improved the lives of many throughout our world. That conviction has been shared by virtually every American president over the years, on both sides of the political spectrum.

To try to address this in limited words, and acknowledging that there are plenty of nuances, research has identified at least three signs that a wholesome patriotic devotion to our country may have turned into something else, reflecting instead a nationalism energized by grievances.

The first sign is when those fellow citizens with whom we disagree are defined as our enemies. In our country, a wholesome patriotism is based upon the belief that people can love our country in different ways and have very diverse ideas about what it needs. Unhealthy nationalism not only denies that normative belief, but also holds the belief that anyone who doesn't share the same view of what's best for the country is a condemnable threat to our country.

The second sign is when politics and religion have become completely blended. Then, political ideology is equated with God's plan, and a culture war then becomes a holy war. It makes political discourse impossible, intrudes into Sunday worship, and is antithetical to Christian beliefs.

The third sign is when our public activities are energized by fear and anger, and our darker emotions of contempt and rage define our political engagement. Our cultural norms call us to be respectful of political opponents in order to continue engaging in the American experiment. That norm is violated when one side demands that other perspectives be vilified or silenced in the public square.

Finally, there can be no such thing as "Christian nationalism." This quote by the conservative Christian author and theologian, Joshua Straub, identifies why that is true: "If the fruit of my political stance is loving those who think like me and hating those who don't: fighting for a policy more than listening to people; padding my pockets before giving to the poor; living in fear more than faith; and loving my country more than my neighbor, then I'm putting trust in this kingdom more than His [Jesus']."

We have lived it before. It is possible to live in peace with those who voted differently than you. It is possible to be friends with someone who views the world differently than you. It is possible to love someone with whom you disagree. Alexis de Tocqueville said it best: "The greatness of America lies not in being more enlightened than any other nation, but rather in her ability to repair her faults." This is such a time.

COMPASSION TOWARD OTHERS

Our inhumanity toward one another popped up again in my thoughts in the last few weeks. Public discussions about diversity and inclusion have surfaced as antisemitic comments and behaviors toward some in our Jewish community have again been promoted. The rise in antisemitism is in the national news. It is again noteworthy that the United Nations, in 2005, established January 27 to be the Holocaust Memorial Day, as a means of remembering the millions of Jews and minority groups who were murdered in the 1930s and 1940s by the Nazis. The day's purpose is to encourage discussion of this very difficult subject with the hope that it will never happen again.

A second thought of mine was about humans and our ability to kill members of our own species. I found out that *Homo sapiens* actually are thirtieth out of more than a thousand species on the list of animals that most often kill members of their own kind. Among primates, we are about in the middle of what turns out to be a particularly violent group. We seem to have an innate tendency toward violence, including toward people just like us. What causes this violence to be committed, and how can we control it?

What causes it to be acted out? According to in-group out-group theory, when we feel threatened by perceived outsiders, we instinctively turn toward our in-group (those with whom we identify) as a survival mechanism. The resulting hatred is driven by two key emotions: love for the in-group and aggression for the out-group. Freud coined the term "projection" to describe a second possible cause: our tendency to reject what we don't like about ourselves and project that "badness" to others by showing hate and judgment towards them.

Psychologist Bernard Golden believes that when hate involves participation in a group, it may help foster a sense of connection or camaraderie that fills a void in one's identity. The person filled with hate may believe that the only way to regain some sense of redress for the pain hate causes is to preemptively strike out at others. Finally, violence and hate may be due to societal and cultural factors such as family history and our cultural and political history. We live in a culture where competition is a way of life, where a culture of war promotes violence, where we are taught to hate the enemy (anyone different from us), and where we are more ready to fight than to peacefully resolve conflict.

What can we do? Hatred is learned. While we are all born with a capacity for violence and aggression, we are also born with a capacity for compassion. Which tendency we adopt requires that a choice be made, individually, in families, in communities, and in our culture in general. The main process in overcoming hate with compassion is education: at home, in our schools, and in our community.

Teaching, learning, and practicing compassion. It often requires us to face the fear of being vulnerable and utterly human in order to connect, to feel, and ultimately, to love. In other words, compassion towards others is the true context that heals hatred. As the sainted comedian George Burns said, "I'd rather be a failure at something I love than a success at something I hate." The Holocaust Memorial Day 2023: a day to remember the Holocaust, to discuss the effects of hate, and to promote compassion.

SECTION IV

COMMON SENSE THINKING ABOUT EDUCATION

ed·u·ca·tion ˌe-jə-ˈkā-shən : the action or process of educating or of being educated *also*: a stage of such a process: the knowledge and development resulting from the process of being educated: the field of study that deals mainly with methods of teaching and learning in schools

NO ONE HAS A MONOPOLY ON TRUTH OR WISDOM

One of the primary goals of all education is to pass on to the next generations the accumulated truths and wisdom that have brought us to this point. In our time, most truths are empirical in nature, often tempered by culture and religion and bias. In any case, it is a good time to remember the role that humility plays in search of truth and wisdom. It was US Supreme Court Justice Elena Kagan, speaking about the importance of learning, who said, 'I've led a school whose faculty and students examine and discuss and debate every aspect of our law and legal system. And what I've learned most is that no one has a monopoly on truth or wisdom. I've learned that we make progress by listening to each other, across every apparent political or ideological divide."

Truth is defined as "a fact or belief that is accepted as true." Until the late sixteenth century, everyone believed the "truth" that the sun and planets revolved around the Earth. Until the late nineteenth century, it was "absolutely true" that epidemic illnesses such as cholera and the plague were caused by a poisonous mist filled with particles from rotting things. And for thousands of years before the early twentieth century, the most common procedure performed by surgeons was bloodletting, because the "truth" was that blood drained from the body balanced the four "humors": blood, phlegm, yellow bile, and black bile. To this day, there are those who believe the "truth" is that former President Obama is a Muslim and was not born in the USA; or that the press is "the enemy of the people." Some also believe that it is "true" that there is no global warming. We are living in a time of such remarkable science and technology and, in spite of it, some stand firmly behind their "truths" … even if so much of what they know to be "true" is actually wrong.

Wisdom is defined as "the quality of having experience, knowledge, and good judgment; the quality of being wise." Well, here are just a few examples of conventional wisdom in the past:

"Louis Pasteur's theory of germs is ridiculous fiction." —Pierre Pachet, Professor of Physiology at Toulouse, 1872.

"I think there is a world market for maybe five computers." —Thomas J. Watson, chairman of the board of IBM, 1943.

"With over 50 foreign cars already on sale here, the Japanese auto industry isn't likely to carve out a big slice of the US market." —*Business Week*, 1958.

"The ordinary 'horseless carriage' is at present a luxury for the wealthy; and although its price will probably fall in the future, it will never, of course, come into as common use as the bicycle." — *Literary Digest*, 1899.

"This 'telephone' has too many shortcomings to be seriously considered as a means of communication. The device is inherently of no value to us." —Western Union internal memo, 1876.

You get the point.

So as another academic year begins, whether you are a student, parent of a student, or neither, it is good to remember that both truth and wisdom are often relative to time, culture, experience, social class, and education. In our moment of time, much of our "truth and wisdom" have become corrupted and twisted by media framing and political meddling. Humility, or recognizing that "no one has a monopoly on truth or wisdom," is a good characteristic to always pursue in seeking the common good; seek those sources of truth and wisdom that provide benefits to our society as a whole rather than to the private good of individuals and sections of society.

AS OUR SCHOOL YEAR COMES TO A CLOSE...

Here is the basic assumption upon which the rest of this thought is based: in the school-based educational complex (excluding the role of parents—which is primary), students are most important and are aided by two levels of servants. The first level of "student servers" is teachers/aids, and the second level of "student/teacher servers" is the administrators.

First, profound changes are taking place in the educational process that primarily impact our teachers—those who are that first line of "servers" for students. Those profound changes come in the form of the technology that is driving innovation, changing the way that students think and, as a result, changing the way that teachers teach.

Digital literacy has become the norm in our nation's schools. As a result, teachers are beginning to take a different approach to education in order to accommodate the needs of 21st-century students. They're integrating technology into instruction by encouraging students to use computers for research or work with adaptive learning (Google it!) technology to grasp new concepts.

Clearly, technology isn't just helping students evolve—it's also changing the role of our teachers in the classroom. To be an excellent teacher now, one has to have mastered certain skills that educators in the past never even had to consider. Here are some examples: 1) instead of telling students what they need to know, teachers now allow students to question what they are learning and to think critically, allowing for more direct interaction with students; 2) teachers now must also be willing to collaborate with students in ways they haven't before, giving them more one-on-one attention and encouraging them to actively engage in the learning process; 3) teachers have to adapt to a totally new perspective on learning, recognizing that 21st-century education is not one-size-fits-all, but that having the ability to tweak curricula, change lesson plans, or open up discussions depending upon the needs and interests of students is essential in the learning process, rather than wholly separate entities; and finally 4) teachers now need to be facilitators of learning, helping students discover knowledge on their own rather than simply imparting it, and placing students in an active role that keeps them engaged and interested in a world that is rapidly changing.

Consequently, the results of a recently published study based in Wisconsin are a bit troublesome. The study showed the following: 1) during a 10-year period, there was a 7 percent increase in students and a 30 percent increase in administrators and other non-teaching staff; 2) if the number of administrators and non-teaching staff (47,196) had increased at the same rate as that of students, the number would be 8,348; 3) if the number of administrators and non-teaching staff had increased at the same rate as students, it would have saved the state of Wisconsin $333,931,797.00; 4) had this same ratio been consistent during these years, each classroom would have saved $9,555 annually and each teacher could have received an annual raise of $5,622. Sometimes it is important to question our priorities.

Along with those realities, the thought still remains about the difficult work teachers have to do with very limited staffing. Please, please commend your child's (children's) teacher(s) as they work hard to prepare the next generation of a world still in the making. Thank you, teachers!

HORACE WHO?

January 24 marks the International Day of Education. This UN commemoration seeks to raise awareness about the importance of education and to create more inclusive, safe, and sustainable societies with education and learning at their centers. The UN notes that currently there are almost 620 million children and youth in our world that lack basic mathematics and literacy skills. We are reminded that "education offers children a way out of poverty and improves their chances of having a promising future."

There are almost twice as many children in the world without access to a good education as there are total people in the USA. We do have problems in our schools, such as excessive class sizes, bullying, teacher retention, student health, and decreased funding. But schools dot our countryside and now, locally and elsewhere, some parents are challenging school boards about what is being taught. Specifically, non-existent courses on critical race theory and concern about aspects of our history are raising tempers and questions.

Sometimes history repeats itself. Horace Mann (1796-1859) served as secretary of the Massachusetts State Board of Education, served as a US representative from 1848-1853, was the founder of

124

Framingham State University, and was the first President of Antioch College. He challenged the status quo of his time by insisting: 1) that ignorance and freedom cannot coexist, so universal education is a necessity; 2) that education needed to be paid for, governed, and regulated by an interested public; 3) that education is best where schools welcome children of all social, ethnic, and religious backgrounds; 4) that education is always moral in character but free of sectarian religious influence; 5) that education must be infused by the discipline, methods, and spirit of a free society; and 6) that education can be provided only by well-trained and professional teachers.

And now the part about history repeating itself. Horace Mann encountered strong resistance to those ideas. The clergy detested nonsectarian schools, thinking the church was the rightful teacher of children and youth. The educators condemned his pedagogy as subversive of classroom authority, since he believed that personal development was more important than disciplinary training. The politicians who opposed the State Board of Education defined it as an improper infringement of local educational authority. Parents thought public education elevated educators above parents and gave the state improper authority over parental rights. But Horace Mann's views about public education prevailed and remain the predominant views to this day.

Finally, a couple of thoughts as we reflect on the International Day of Education. It was Thomas Jefferson who, believing that the poor and rich had to have equal access to a good education, proposed that the state pay for universal primary education as well as fund education at later stages. He was also opposed by many, especially those wary of big government or higher taxes. It is interesting, therefore, to remember that one of his most enthusiastic supporters was an old political opponent and friend, the conservative John Adams. "The whole people must take upon themselves the education of the whole people and must be willing to bear the expenses of it," Adams wrote. "There should not be a district of one mile square, without a school in it, not founded by a charitable individual, but maintained at the public expense of the people." Thank you to the many who came before us and to those among us today who encourage, support, and implement public education.

NATIONAL TEACHER'S DAY

May 5 is National Teachers Day, originated through the work of Eleanor Roosevelt, a teacher herself. In 1953, she first requested that Congress honor teachers with a designated nation recognition day, but the first National Teacher's Day did not become an official national day until 1980.

Prior to Teacher's Day becoming officially recognized, it was President John F. Kennedy who said that "modern cynics and skeptics see no harm in paying those to whom they entrust the minds of their children a smaller wage than is paid to those to whom they entrust the care of their plumbing." Sixty years later, things have remained much the same. Underpaying our teachers for work that requires well-recognized high responsibilities has been a long-standing condition. In fact, it seems to have accelerated even as we have "dumped" more and more parental responsibilities on them. Without asking for the additional responsibilities, schools and teachers find themselves with cultural responsibility for the physical health, nutrition, discipline, safety, values, and mental health of other people's children. As American entrepreneur John Sculley said, "We expect teachers to handle teenage pregnancy, substance abuse, and the failings of the family. Then we expect them to educate our children." Similar things have also happened to law enforcement (who mostly spend their time as social workers with the most marginal in our society) and other service-oriented professions.

Being a teacher is hard work and the lower the grade levels, the harder the work and the lower the pay. The cultural value-base for work in the USA is hideously inverted, with the positions that offer the most in providing for important cultural needs receiving the lowest pay and, too often, status. Perhaps that is why former President Obama said about teaching that "by the end of two years, most have either changed careers or moved to suburban schools – a consequence of low pay, a lack of support from the educational bureaucracy, and a pervasive feeling of isolation."

As we reflect on teachers and teaching, however, it is good also to reflect on what the noted psychiatrist, Dr. Karl Menninger, said. In his view, "What the teacher is, is more important than what he/she teaches." Consistent throughout a half-century or more of research is the reality that the most important factor in any child's education is the perception that one's teacher likes the student. Feeling that your teacher likes you is much more important than facilities, programs, processes, and all of the other "stuff" that makes up current education. We can argue about a lot of things with regard to teachers, but if they do not like each individual student, the future prospects of the disliked student are diminished. So we are called to be discerning about teachers, and to hold accountable those that are ill-equipped by disposition or training to be teachers. Nonetheless, since they are the primary profession to pass on to the next generation the accumulated wisdom of our culture, we should surely honor, support, encourage, and reward them for perhaps the most important of all cultural roles. Remember them on May 5.

"MY DEAR CHILDREN"

My dear children: I rejoice to see you before me today, happy youth of a sunny and fortunate land. Bear in mind that the wonderful things that you learn in your schools are the work of many generations, produced by enthusiastic effort and infinite labor in every country of the world. All this is put into your hands as your inheritance in order that you may receive it, honor it, and add to it, and one day faithfully hand it on to your children. Thus do we mortals achieve immortality in the permanent things which we create in common. If you always keep that in mind you will find meaning in life and work and acquire the right attitude towards other nations and ages. —Albert Einstein, 1934

I entered kindergarten exactly seventy-nine years ago, was a reluctant and quite cynical student from the beginning, and remained suspicious about conventional "wisdom" while plodding through six degrees (college, university, seminary). Often I was on the bandwagon for change, and even succeeded sometimes in helping to bring it about. So I thought that maybe this is the time to invest in some reflection and share what I have experienced about education over those years as a student, teacher, professor, and administrator.

- As research has demonstrated for at least fifty years, the most important single ingredient in a successful school experience for a student is *having a teacher who likes and encourages you.*
- The only important factors with regard to facilities are *light* and *clean air.* The rest, while nice "value-addeds," are relatively unimportant to learning.
- *Hard work* is still the only way to accomplish great learning. No one is entitled to anything unless they have expended the commensurate amount of work to accomplish it.
- The *best administrators are those who teach while administering,* and the second best are those who come from teaching and return to it after a time as an administrator.
- Division between teachers and administrators has increased as administrators changed from a public service model to a CEO/corporate model of leadership.
- The best school principals are those who are chosen by the teachers they serve.
- *Maximum autonomy* for teachers produces the best teaching.
- *Maximum parental cooperation* on behalf of and in encouraging children is critical to success.
- *Schools aren't social work agencies.* Parents are still best equipped to handle matters of health, discipline, values-sharing, etc. Over the past thirty-plus years, many parents have abdicated these responsibilities, and schools have had to fill the gaps.

Space limitations require me to stop identifying learnings at this point. I'm sure you have your own to share. In the meanwhile, reread the words of Dr. Einstein above, and reflect on the truths he shares. Have a great school year!

A SCHOOL TEACHER, THE STATE OF WISCONSIN, AND NATIONAL FLAG DAY!

June 14 often passes largely unnoticed. Nonetheless, it is an important day. It is National Flag Day! Did you know that the use of flags as a symbol dates back to the Zhou dynasty in China (1046-256 BC)? Did you know that on June 14, 1877, the Stars and Stripes was officially accepted as our national flag? And did you know that it was in 1885 that the idea of an annual day specifically celebrating our flag is believed to have first originated? A teacher in Wisconsin by the name of Bernard J. Cigrand arranged for the pupils in the Fredonia Public School, District 6, to observe June 14 as "Flag Birthday." In many newspaper articles and magazines, as well as in public addresses over the following years, he continued enthusiastically to endorse and advocate for the observance of June 14 as "Flag Birthday" or "Flag Day."

As often happens, however, it took many decades of various types of celebrations in diverse parts of our country before Flag Day was officially recognized. It was President Woodrow Wilson who issued a proclamation declaring May 30, 1916, to be Flag Day. After that, Flag Day was celebrated in many communities throughout the USA for years, even though it had not been officially designated by an act of Congress. It was finally on August 3, 1949, that President Harry S.

Truman signed a bill designating June 14 of each year as National Flag Day.

But what Montaigne (1553-1592) said remains true, namely, "There never were in the world two opinions alike, no more than two hairs or two grains; the most universal quality is diversity." And surely there is diversity of opinion about how we are to treat our flag and whether we are required to stand in its presence or salute it or pledge allegiance to it. As President Herbert Hoover said, however, "Honest difference of views and honest debate are not disunity. They are the vital process of policy among free men."

So for some good citizens among us, some of the most harmful things in this world and in our country seem to come in shades of red, white, and blue. And it is true that in 247 years of independence, the United States has often fallen short of its values and ideals. Nonetheless, it is those values and ideals that our flag symbolizes or embodies, not our failure to live up to them. Showing respect to our flag is not to proclaim that America can do no wrong, but to believe in its great capacity to do right. A very important part of that "capacity to do right" is to recognize and affirm that it is also a fundamental American value and ideal (see the First Amendment to our Constitution) to speak out when those values have been violated. We are often confronted with the question of whether we stand with our governmental policies or take our stand as the loyal opposition. Certainly, the US is always our country, but that does not mean we are to go along with what is wrong. As Albert Camus (1913-1960), the noted philosopher, said, "I should be able to love my country and still love justice."

On Flag Day we remember that we are a government "of ... by ... and for the people," as Abraham Lincoln said. That means that policies are debated in the public forum as well as in the halls of Congress. To deny differences of opinion and to brand some as unpatriotic are to squelch the very behavior by which democracy lives and breathes. So pledge to the flag or salute the flag if your patriotic spirit calls you to do so, or don't if your patriotic spirit calls you not to. Why? Because we can't be compelled to do either. That's been true since 1943, when the US Supreme Court ruled in the case of *West Virginia State Board of Education* v. *Barnette* that individuals couldn't be forced to salute the US flag or say the pledge, because that would violate their First Amendment rights. "If there is any fixed star in our constitutional constellation, it is that no official, high or petty, can prescribe what shall be orthodox in politics, nationalism, religion, or other matters of opinion, or force citizens to confess by word or act their faith therein," Justice Robert Jackson wrote in the majority opinion. Or as Justice Brennan said, "We do not consecrate the flag by punishing its desecration, for in doing so, we dilute the freedom this cherished emblem represents." A good closing thought on Flag Day.

IT SHOULD END THERE

I t again seems to be a small but noisy part of the people we are. At least since the 1640s, we have practiced book banning. My own view is quite circumscribed in this regard. I agree with Clare Booth Luce (1903-1987, an American writer, Republican politician, US ambassador, and public conservative figure) when she said that "censorship, like charity, should begin at home; but unlike charity, it should end there."

In 1624, an English businessman named Thomas Morton debarked in Massachusetts. He arrived with a group of Puritans, and very soon learned that the strict rules and social values by which they lived were difficult for him to live with. He decided to just move and set up his own colony, now known as the City of Quincy, MA. There, people lived by the forbidden customs from the Old World that the Puritans found to be abhorrent. After being exiled by the Puritan militia, Morton sued them and wrote a book (*New English Canaan*, 1637) attacking Puritan customs and calling the Puritans wood lice, water fleas, and barnacles. Even the liberal New England settlers did not approve of the book. Anyway, the Puritans banned it, likely making it the first book banned in the United States.

Throughout our history, very large numbers of books have been banned or challenged. It once led Benjamin Franklin to say that "whoever would overthrow the liberty of a nation must begin by subduing the freeness of speech." While censorship has a long history among us, the fight against it began forty-one years ago. In 1982, in *Island Trees School District* v. *Pico* the Supreme Court ruled that school officials cannot ban books solely based on their content. As a result of that ruling and in that same year, organizers at the American Booksellers Association's BookExpo America trade show in Anaheim, California, developed a plan to highlight the banning of books in our nation. Because of the implementation of that plan, major news outlets and local politicians started taking notice and publicly proclaiming their support. The result was that Banned Books Week was born.

Now here's an interesting discovery. According to research by Laura Juraska, a librarian at Bates College in Maine, books are banned for different reasons, all depending on which part of our planet you are living. Here in the United States, we are most likely to ban books about sex and religion. Elsewhere, banned books are most often about politics. As she says, "It tells you something about the culture that we live in." Banning books about sex and religion? What about 14,000 gun deaths so far in 2023, and living in an "open carry" state? Why no banning of weapons of war? In Wisconsin, 640,000 people are living in poverty. Why no banning of poverty? Also in Wisconsin, there were 494,939 drunken driving convictions last year. Why is there no banning of alcohol? We live in a world on the edge of climate disaster. Why no banning of fossil fuels? The words still ring in my ears from my third grade teacher, "Okay boys and girls, time now to put on your thinking caps." Good advice as we are again in an era of book banning and other follies.

"ANGER IS AN ACID ...."

"Anger is an acid that can do more harm to the vessel in which it is stored than to anything on which it is poured," said Mark Twain. The mood of our country remains mean-spirited. Our public discourse and our private social relationships too often become increasingly hostile and angry. Anger is now regularly demonstrated in Hudson's Common Council and School Board meetings. Part of this anger is still related to many of the changes in the world around us that challenge our security, stability, individuality, and comfort. Some of it is an expected part of such change.

But what I am speaking of here is not the anger associated with normal change inherent within our society, but the orchestrated and professionally engineered anger that has become a part of both our public and private conversations. You can crisscross this country and see the same slogans shared in the same tone about the same issues that have come to provide the power base for some. You can ask almost anyone on the streets and in similar language and with similar anger hear the ranting and railing about some of our elected leaders and their political, economic, and social policies that seem very much out of proportion to the reality at hand. Most of this has been accomplished by using communication strategies, and particularly propaganda devices, that distort, manipulate, mislead, deceive, and even coerce our fellow citizens.

When did the amount of cultural anger begin to change? Whether you review the past Gallup polls or the Pew Research Center's polling over the years, they both seem to agree that the trend began in the 1970s when the political conversations in Washington became divisive. Recent academic research confirms what those polls tell us. Last year, two university political science professors published an international study about "affective polarization," the way we feel about the opposite political party. They found that in 1978, we rated people who belonged to our own political party twenty-seven points higher than people who belonged to the other party. While the trend toward increased anger toward the opposite political party and its adherents was fairly slow at first, in the year 2000 it began to spike. By 2016, it had gone up to forty-five points – the highest by far of any of the countries surveyed – and that is before the 2017-2020 timeframe, which was the most highly politically divisive.

It is true that anger can provide healthy as well as shortsighted and self-destructive consequences. Anger can create a sense of power and control in some situations. It can motivate you to challenge and change difficult interpersonal and social injustices. If you are a dedicated reformer working to further a truly moral cause (such as Martin Luther King, Jr.'s drive for civil rights, or John Lewis's drive for voting rights), then anger can give you the strength and the will to persevere.

But there are negative motivational sides to anger, too. Negative anger can initiate and then reinforce a false sense of entitlement and the illusion of moral superiority that can be used to justify immoral actions. It can motivate aggression that can be used to justify terrorism. Such people often subscribe to the philosophy that "the end justifies the means" and use unspeakable means to achieve their goals. As they allow negative anger to motivate them to coerce and control others, they are no better than a bully.

The advice that Mr. Rogers gave to our children remains good advice still for us in our adulthood: "We all have negative urges, but we don't have to act out those urges." An alternative, according to the prophet Isaiah, is to remember and practice the reality that "in quietness and confidence shall be your strength." (Isaiah 30:15)

EARTH MONTH: OUR PLANET, OUR STATE, OUR CITY

OUR PLANET

It has been fifty-three years since Wisconsin's Senator Gaylord Nelson provided the idea and impetus to begin what became known as "Earth Day." Over the years we have disagreed with our role in protecting our part of this small planet. Some think our planet is ours to use and abuse until spent; others think it is our responsibility to pass it on to the next generation in equal or better shape than we received it. Many, I think, remain apathetic or unthinking about it. The theme for Earth Day 2023 (April 22) is "Invest in our Planet" to "preserve and protect our health, our families, our livelihoods." Reflecting on this theme, I hope we can all be renewed in our desires to live the tag line that implores us to "Think Globally – Act Locally."

OUR STATE

The Arbor Day movement began in the 1800s to promote conservation and beautification of the environment. It began in the Nebraska Territory, at a meeting of the Board of Agriculture, when a newspaper editor, J. Sterling Morton, first proposed a tree-planting holiday to be called "Arbor Day." Arbor Day is a Wisconsin School Observance Day and national observance day to encourage people to plant and care for trees. Since enacted into law in Wisconsin on May 7, 1980 (1979 Laws of Wisconsin, Chapter 214), it has been observed on the last Friday in April.

OUR CITY

Hudson, Wisconsin, has been a "Tree City" since 2010. Founded by the Arbor Day Foundation in 1976, the Tree City USA program provides assistance and recognition to Hudson since it maintains a continuously active tree management program. To achieve Tree City USA status, Hudson is required to meet four core standards of urban forestry management: maintaining a tree department, having a community tree ordinance, spending at least $2 per capita on urban forestry, and celebrating Arbor Day.

We have come a long way in fifty-three years in our appreciation for and celebration of our planet. Earth Day is now widely recognized as the largest secular observance in the world, celebrated by more than a billion people every year as a day of action. We all can only do what we can do, but on this Earth Day think about what you do now and what you are capable of. It is good to be encouraged to stretch into your true ability to promote the health of our planet and then just do what you can do. Senator Gaylord Nelson observed, "The wealth of the nation is its air, water, soil, forests, minerals, rivers, lakes, oceans, scenic beauty, wildlife habitats, and biodiversity." That is surely true for our planet, our state, and our city. Enjoy and protect our wealth. Happy Earth Day.

SECTION V

COMMON SENSE THINKING ABOUT THE ECONOMY

econ·o·my i-ˈkä-nə-mē : the structure or conditions of economic life in a country, area, or period *also* : an economic system: thrifty and efficient use of material resources : frugality in expenditures *also* : an instance or a means of economizing: efficient and concise use of nonmaterial resources (such as effort, language, or motion): the arrangement or mode of operation of something: a system especially of interaction and exchange.

WHY IS IT SO SCARY?

We seem always to be in the midst of another insufferably long election season. Mostly, we are focused on the presidential race, a challenge to any level reality at a minimum. Thus far, we have heard the candidates called "idiots," "freaks," "clowns," "messes," and, worst of all in the eyes of some, "democratic socialist"!

What is so scary about being a *democratic* (supporting democracy and its principles) *socialist* (believing that the most harmonious state of affairs would be for all to get a fair shot at financial success)? I simply do not know. A democratic socialist believes and supports the idea that both the economy and society should be run democratically, in a manner such that the needs of the public are addressed, rather than to make profits for a few. Democratic socialists think that ordinary American citizens should be able to participate in the many decisions that affect their lives.

This is nothing new. Democracy and socialism go hand in hand. All over the world, wherever the idea of democracy has taken root, the vision of socialism has taken root as well. Everywhere, that is, but in the United States during the past few decades. Instead, we have allowed a non-democratic form of socialism to emerge. Instead of "we the people" deciding what aspects of social caring and economic investments we want to share, large corporate bureaucracies, a few huge banks, and even fewer extremely rich families now make most of the basic economic and social decisions that affect almost all of the rest of us. Democratic socialists believe that social and economic decisions should be made by those whom they most affect.

It is good to note that democratic socialists have long rejected the belief that the whole economy and social structure should be centrally planned by the government. Rather, they recognize that there are some social and economic matters that are best addressed by "we the people" than by the few rich and powerful with strong self-interests. In short, democratic planning by means of the democratic processes can shape major social and economic investments like education, mass transit, fire and police protection, housing, healthcare, and energy, to name a few. Because democratic socialism has been practiced in our country in the past, we now have public education, public roads, Social Security, Medicare, fire and police protection, the right to vote, free elections, and almost innumerable other processes and practices that serve the good of "we the people." What is so scary about that?

"STUCK ON STUPID"

Okay … so I know that Chris Brown has a song entitled "Stuck on Stupid," but my reason for using that phrase has quite a different origin. On a recent Sunday in church I was sitting beside another "regular," and I asked where he was from (Cincinnati) and then how he got to St. Paul, MN (he fell in love with a "Woman in the Airforce" who was from St. Paul), and finally, how different St. Paul was in the early 1960s. At that time, the city was alive with streetcars, trolleys, electric busses, etc. All were eliminated shortly thereafter as cars became the normative vehicle of choice, and the rest is history. Now it is costing hundreds of times as much to begin to return to a more eco-friendly and efficient means of public transportation. In short, he defined the many cultural and political decisions we have made in the last forty years as being "stuck on stupid." For example, in a recent report the American Society of Civil Engineers gives our country a D+ in how we have taken care of our infrastructural needs. In the next five years, we need to spend $3.6 trillion just to bring them up to a reasonable standard (for comparison, we will spend almost the same amount in the next five years for military and veterans' needs). Here in Wisconsin, 71 percent of our roads are in poor or mediocre condition, we have 1,232 structurally deficient bridges, and we have 157 high-hazard dams, etc.

Of course, there are many more "stupid" things we have accomplished: 1) The United States is now the most unequal in distribution of wealth among all the advanced economies of the world and near the bottom when compared with all the countries of the world. In fact, the 0.1 percent who together possess over a quarter of all wealth (28 percent), possess more wealth than the combined holdings of 310 million Americans — 95 percent of us; 2) The United States is the only advanced economy that doesn't guarantee paid vacation and one of only thirteen countries in the world not to do so, according to the World Policy Analysis Center at the University of California Los Angeles; 3) In 2023, according to the Commonwealth Fund, the USA is again ranked highest in cost and lowest in quality among the ten most comparable countries, namely and in order: a) United Kingdom, b) Switzerland, c) Sweden, d) Australia, e) Germany and the Netherlands (tied), f) New Zealand & Norway (tied), g) France, h) Canada, and i) United States. More specifically, health spending per person in the US was nearly two times higher than in Canada. In the US, that includes spending for people in public programs like Medicaid, the Children's Health Insurance Program, Medicare, and military plans; spending by those with private employer-sponsored coverage or other private insurance; and out-of-pocket health spending.

And surely there are easily dozens more examples, but perhaps the best constructive reminder as we are about to begin a new year under new leadership in the US House and Senate is the reminder from Theodore Roosevelt that "in any moment of decision, the best thing you can do is the right thing. The worst thing you can do is nothing." Change is difficult, but not changing is disastrous.

IT DEPENDS ON WHAT YOU CALL IT!

In a business that we recently sold, our tagline was "Less About Me, More About We." Over ten years ago we already had a significant sense that the "we" that is required for a democracy to exist had been demonized and that the very foundations of our country were at risk. I say that because the essence of the "American Dream" is the shared perspective that everyone in our country has agreed to the kind of relationships with others that adheres to the ideals that are greater than us. We agreed that the truths embodied in those ideals were so "self-evident" (Declaration of Independence, July 4, 1776) that they would comprise the foundation of our journey together "toward a more perfect union." Of course, it was understood that there would always be some respectful disagreements on the journey. Because of that, we also agreed that the responsibility and authority to govern and arbitrate such disagreements would come from "we the people."

Unfortunately, in my judgment, we have come to the moment when the "we" of our society is really no longer a "we." "We" no longer seem to share the basic values and truths to which we subscribed in the Declaration of Independence and in the Constitution which followed. When "we" no longer share these basic truths, "we" no longer have legitimate authority, and have nothing to unify us and help us maintain our continuing association in pursuit of a dream no longer shared.

While this topic deserves a long treatise, I would suggest that how we name and define important cultural realities is a part of the problem. So as a beginning in reminding ourselves that "we the people" have agreed that pursuing life, liberty, and happiness are "self-evident," here are some suggested name changes that might unite us:

Regulations: This has become a negative and divisive term, so how about *protections* instead? That is, of course, the purpose of having regulations – to protect us from harmful things.

Taxes: Another negative and divisive term. So how about *civic contributions*, since that is what we have agreed to do: join together to collectively pay for services that benefit us all.

Government: Really? Why has this term become a negative? How about *civic service*, since we elect citizens from among us to represent us in working toward fulfilling our agreed-upon "self-evident" values.

Well, enough for these comments. How about just committing to memory the phrase "less about me, more about we" and renewing your efforts to live by that motto? Thanks, fellow citizen.

AFRAID OF THE LIGHT

I t was Plato (427-347 BC) who said that "we can easily forgive a child who is afraid of the dark; the real tragedy of life is when people are afraid of the light."

There have been numerous periods throughout human history when people in public and powerful positions have used fear to inflict their will or ideology upon their fellow citizens. We are living through a period of history now where in many parts of the world, including the United States of America, the specter of fear seems prevalent in our public and private discussions – the fear of terrorists, of government, of elected officials, of Muslims, of Mexicans, of Republicans, of Democrats, of protestors … and the list goes on and on.

It is true that we are living in a time of significant economic and cultural insecurity. Economically, an exceedingly small minority owns more wealth than a very huge majority, and such income inequality continues to grow. According to Forbes and others, for example, the one-tenth of 1 percent (0.1 percent) together possess over a quarter of all wealth (28 percent), which is more wealth than the combined holdings of 310 million Americans (95 percent of all of us). Culturally, we are in a state of flux as mass migrations of peoples cross borders due to war or famine, simply seeking a peaceful and productive life elsewhere. According to the World Bank, 215 million people, or 3.05 percent of the world population, are living in a country other than their country of origin. Almost all were seeking a better life for themselves and their families.

While the causes of these economic and cultural insecurities are complex, they are the primary root causes of fear. It is therefore important that we seek to find and implement radical (meaning "getting to the root of the problem") solutions to replacing fear with "light."

Part of the answer for those of us in the USA may be to again study, reflect upon, and then draw upon the power of our historic and Constitutional ideals. Continuing to take the risks of developing and supporting new and sustainable technology, a more equitable prosperity, and a more just manner in which we conduct business and commerce will do more than xenophobia ("fear of the stranger") to banish people's insecurities. In addition, one way to overcome resentment is through just and equitable economic growth—not by putting up walls. One way to defeat Islamist terrorism is to enlist the help of Muslims, instead of treating them as hostile enemies. Fifty-five years ago, shortly before his assassination, Robert Kennedy said that "ultimately, America's answer to the intolerant [person] is diversity." You, I, and surely the political parties and elected officials we support need to make that case loudly and convincingly.

Here is the most personal part of all – the choice ultimately falls to us as voters, and most of us do not subscribe to the rule of fear. But the voter turnout for primaries and caucuses and elections in America is troubling. According to Pew research, in 2020, only 66.5 percent of registered voters voted in this past presidential election year. On a list of thirty of the world's most developed nations, the USA is in seventeenth place in voter turnout. I hope you will forgive me for saying, "That is shameful!" The way to beat the rule of fear begins at the ballot box. The moderate, positive, inclusive, and optimistic majority has a responsibility to show up and put a mark next to candidates who stand for openness and tolerance as an antidote to fear. As we are closing out an old year and about to begin a new year, it is good to be reminded by former President Theodore Roosevelt that "in any moment of decision, the best thing you can do is the right thing. The worst thing you can do is nothing." Change is difficult; not changing can be disastrous. Fear is disabling, while enlightenment can be compelling.

BEING AN ENTREPRENEUR

We have entered the month of March, the third month of the year and the first month of spring in our hemisphere. It was named after the Roman god, Mars. March was the first month in the early Roman calendar, signifying fresh starts and new beginnings. We, too, are having new beginnings and fresh starts. The fears of the pandemic are being reduced, the economy is getting much stronger, and small and big business start-ups are increasing. I have been defined for this column as a small business owner. As such, and since the Millennial, Generation Z, and Generation X cohorts have different perspectives about business, a review of an alternate business model that better meets their expectations may be helpful.

The dictionary defines an entrepreneur as a "risk-taking businessperson: somebody who initiates or finances new commercial enterprises." The predominant business model is that of a business entrepreneur. A more recent and alternative business model is that of a social entrepreneur. Both models seek to find a gap and create a venture to serve an unserved market. But while the business entrepreneurs' efforts focus on building a business and earning profits, the social entrepreneurs' purpose is to create social change. In summary, a business entrepreneur may create changes in the society, but that is not the primary purpose of starting the venture. Similarly, a social entrepreneur may generate profits, but for him/her that is not the primary reason for starting the venture.

Perhaps this is best summarized in terms of wealth. For the business entrepreneur, 'wealth' is same as profits. For the social entrepreneur, however, wealth also encompasses the creation and sustenance of social and environmental capital. In other words, using the merchandise the social entrepreneur business sells as teaching examples, the customers learn and experience social responsibility and environmental sustainability. Marketing is based upon a "triple bottom line" business model where people, planet, and profits are all equally important.

Social entrepreneurship is a relatively new term in our culture, being just a couple of decades in use. But its practice can be found throughout much of history. Currently, many major brands and companies are adopting the concept of social entrepreneurship and trying to address some of the issues in our society and the world. A portion of the proceeds from sales help to open schools in far flung areas, increase child rights, improve women empowerment, save the environment, save trees, treat waste products, educate girls and women, make it possible for farmers and poor individuals to access low interest loans, and help in the process of going green.

Our younger generations expect businesses to be about more than making money. They expect businesses to be willing partners in making the world a better place to live and thrive. This growing expectation has also encouraged Social Entrepreneurship to be included as a separate branch of management courses in some universities. As a wise sage once said, "people most often change not because they see the light but because they feel the heat." May the younger generations keep the heat on as an aid to businesses becoming more conscious of prioritizing people and our planet as well as profit.

HOW COULD IT BE WORSE?

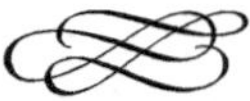

Difficult as it is to comprehend, and based upon current US Census reports, 41.4 percent of Americans are classified as low-income or low-income families. The top 1 percent of earners make 20 times more than the bottom 90 percent, and the 1 percent have drained $50 trillion from the bottom 90 percent over the last 45 years.

Economic inequality produces damage that lasts a lifetime and beyond. That's one reason why in 2013 President Obama said that "increasing inequality … challenges the very essence of who we are as a people." The study above found that the wealth gap between the top 1 percent and the remaining 99 percent keeps getting worse. Earnings for the top 1 percent reached a "new high" that year. The 1 percent's income increase of 7.7 percent was nearly twice everyone else's.

According to the study, "this uneven recovery is unfortunately on par with a long-term widening of inequality since 1980, when the top 1 percent of families began to capture a disproportionate share of economic growth." That was the year Ronald Reagan first took office and the year in which he began a new era of economic conservatism in the United States, often referred to as "trickle-down economics." The message of these numbers couldn't be clearer: it's time for that era to end. Our 35-year experiment with conservative economics has failed the great majority of our fellow citizens.

A society with this kind of extreme and growing inequality will be unable to sustain itself over time. Inequality interferes with economic growth, robs most of our citizens of opportunity and hope, ensures that millions will live in poverty or near-impoverished conditions, and sickens that part of the human spirit that constantly searches for fairness and equality. It also makes the society we love inherently unstable, especially when our political system as currently demonstrated gives extremely wealthy individuals and corporations excessive control over the government. In doing so, it perpetuates and amplifies the wealth and power of the 1 percent at the continuing expense of the 99 percent.

Such economic damage is often carried down the generations, through the children, affecting their health and ability to earn. So what can we do to reduce inequality and heal some of its deep, long-lasting wounds? Here are a few suggestions. We can increase funds for antipoverty programs that provide food, shelter, and other services directly to the poor. We can improve our educational system and provide tuition-free public college to all qualified students. We can address the systemic racial injustice that deprives communities of color of economic resources. We can raise the minimum wage, which has fallen far behind inflation (and even farther behind productivity) since 1968.

In addition, we can also strengthen the labor movement. A recent study by the International Monetary Fund found that a "decline in union density has been strongly associated with the rise of top income inequality" and that "unionization matters for income distribution." We must again work hard to provide health insurance for all and to ensure that all working Americans have access to the paid leave programs and other benefits found in other developed countries.

The Fourth of July has come and gone. Another national election awaits us. As you research the candidates, please consider the many scars of inequality that are still here, depriving millions of us of the freedom to choose, to grow, and even to live. And please vote.

HONESTY AND WISDOM

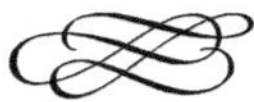

At one of my last birthdays, our daughters gave me one of those services where I am sent a new question each week for a year about something in my life. At the end of the year, I will have written an autobiography based on those questions. One of the recent questions asked about growing up in the small Iowa town in which I then lived. A part of my response to that question says that "I do not remember being divided into the 'haves' and 'have-nots,' into liberal or conservative, or into ethnicities. Instead, we were all together experiencing World War II, the polio epidemic, the Korean War, rationing, and the threat of an atomic bomb ... so there were plenty of activities that unified us instead of dividing us. All in all, a good 'neighborhood' in which to grow up and learn the importance of 'less about me, more about we.'"

Our daughters and their children, on the other hand, passed from childhood into maturity during an approximately fifty-year transitional period of growing inequality and the shattering of economic opportunity. Added to that economic divide, and compounded by it, were and are other divisions in our country, including cultural, racial, religious, and even regional separations. These factors have made it so much more difficult to build consensus on issues, have made politicians less willing to compromise, and have made us even more cynical about politics.

We are just living through the ending of a pandemic. Many of the values and behaviors that came to predominate over these past fifty years are now being questioned. We are once again hearing phrases such as "we're all in this together," even as we continue to divide ourselves over wearing face masks. As we move ahead, hoping that we all reflect on personal changes that would enhance our togetherness, I suggest that we reconsider two values that would aid us in that process. One value is honesty. Public honesty seems to have fallen into disrepute during the past few years. Being honest refers to moral character, integrity, clear-spoken truthfulness, and the absence of cheating, lying, or theft. In virtually all religions and cultures, honesty is revered. It means being fair, trustworthy, loyal, truthful, sincere, and transparent in one's conduct. There is an old proverb that says, "Honesty is the best policy."

But there is a second and related value that is noted by Thomas Jefferson when he said, "Honesty is the first chapter in the book of wisdom." The Roman stoic philosopher, Seneca, said, "No man was ever wise by chance." Developing wisdom takes time and experience. It is the ability to use one's knowledge and intelligence and understanding in such a manner that the choices we make are productive and beneficial, what some call "common sense for the common good." In short, you don't get wisdom out of a textbook or knowledge enough to make you wise. You can't grow in understanding from simply hearing what others say. Experience seems to be the most valuable among the various tools in acquiring wisdom. To paraphrase someone else's words of wisdom: one can hear lectures on swimming, read books on swimming, and understand the buoyancy of water from observation. Until, however, one jumps in the water and gets some experience, one will not have true wisdom about the water, and that may make all the difference between swimming and drowning. Experience is often the best teacher.

We are living through a time for honest re-evaluation about making wise choices and changes. We have an opportunity to transform a cultural system that is filled with profound economic and political inequalities. History sometimes provides unexpected developments that open up opportunities for those bold enough to see and act on them. For the sake of our younger generations particularly, renewing our dedication to honesty and wisdom will aid us in passing on to them a lifestyle that provides common-sense solutions that enhance the common good.

WATCHING WHAT PEOPLE DO

December is the month of Hanukkah, Christmas, and Kwanzaa. This holiday season, perhaps more than others, I again remember the words of Andrew Carnegie who said, "As I grow older, I pay less attention to what [people] say. I just watch what they do." I look at the newspaper ads, the TV ads, and the many and varied social media ads. What I see again is the commercialization of holidays, an open season for marketers.

The "reasons for the season" stand in opposition to the reality. Hanukkah reminds Jews to rededicate themselves to keeping alive the flame of Jewish religion and culture, so that it may be passed on to the next generation. Christmas is a Christian celebration of the birth of Jesus, with time for loved ones to celebrate together the religious teachings and life of Jesus. Kwanzaa is an annual holiday affirming African American families and the social values of unity, self-determination, responsibility, cooperative economics, purpose, creativity, and faith. Those who follow other faiths, or are not religious at all, also feel the effects of reality superseding the reasons for the season.

The ways we celebrate this season dilute the intentions in the origins of Hanukkah, Christmas, and Kwanzaa. That is not to say that we shouldn't celebrate the season. We should. You might, however, be interested in another celebratory day in this season and how it helps to separate the gift-giving from the purpose of the holidays.

December 6 is St. Nicholas Day. St. Nicholas was born around the year AD 280 and lived in Asia Minor, which is now Turkey. During his lifetime, he lived his life as a servant of God. Through his caring kindness and generosity, he became known throughout the world, and he is the patron saint of multiple diverse groups, including children. In many countries, children await anxiously for the morning of December 6th to see if St. Nicholas visited them with gifts during the night.

While the celebration of St. Nicholas Day varies by country, in most cases, the gift-giving in anticipation of Christmas Day is separated from the religious celebration of Jesus' birth. This is just a reminder that all the holiday-themed products or promotions are marketing-based, and the vibrant holiday decorations and cheer would not be present if it did not help sales.

This is a gentle admonition that there are nonmaterial priorities that also accompany the holidays. Unlike most things, they do not have an expiration date and are not limited to one day. They are summarized, in part, by the words so often quoted in Christmas cards: "Peace and good will toward all." It is a time to reflect on being more giving, more caring, more kind, and more respectful of others every day of our lives.

Finally, as we celebrate this holiday season, may we be increasingly filled with love, peace, joy, and hope. May these attributes, accompanied also with kindness and friendship, be not just for our friends and family, but for all the people we meet throughout the coming year. It is a season for generosity, especially for sharing our blessings with others, including those who are less fortunate.

Above all, these holidays are a time for hope and joy. A blessed holiday season to all!

GEORGE ORWELL, AGAIN

George Orwell is best known for writing *1984*, but he also wrote a lesser-known book entitled *Politics and the English Language* (1946). How we use language in connection with political life is the topic he discusses. There have been problematic elements in political language for many decades in the American political realm. Take the word *liberal*, for example. It has been used to vilify others for many decades, including President Kennedy (1917-63), who responded with these words: "If by a 'Liberal' they mean someone who looks ahead and not behind, someone who welcomes new ideas without rigid reactions, someone who cares about the welfare of the people—their health, their housing, their schools, their jobs, their civil rights and their civil liberties—someone who believes we can break through the stalemate and suspicions that grip us in our policies abroad, if that is what they mean by a 'Liberal,' then I'm proud to say I'm a 'Liberal.'" (*Profiles in Courage*, 1955).

The word *liberal* is still used to this day by some to vilify others, even though the meaning of the word is good. It comes from the Latin word *liber*, which means freedom. Currently, the same vilifying process is attached to the word *woke*. While its use has a complicated history, its basic meaning is to be "aware of and actively attentive to important societal facts and issues (especially issues of racial and social justice)."

According to Orwell, the words we use can be both a cause and an effect. If we use imprecise and sloppy language, the way we think also becomes imprecise and sloppy. It becomes easier for us to be inaccurate in our thinking and to use words in a vilifying sense. That is the current problem with using the word *woke*. It is now being used to condemn others and to announce one's anti-woke membership as a badge in a cultural war. Calling something or somebody "woke" is the user's way of expressing unhappiness with how things are, how they would like the world to change to their way of thinking, and inviting others who share their general, inarticulate uneasiness to join them. As Orwell said, "Words of this kind are often used in a consciously dishonest way."

More specifically, declaring others to be "woke" in current public usage often means that "they" are both wrong and enemies of our civilization, and a threat to all that is decent and good. It does seem true that as a nation we both could and would benefit from a genuine conversation and thorough discussion about cultural issues. None-theless, when we use "woke" as a catchall term for everything that is deemed to be bad, it is not helpful. Rather, it almost always adds to our current political confusion and conflict.

Maybe George Orwell was correct. Our political lives and practice of politics could be improved by improving the language we use. He closed by saying that "if one gets rid of these habits, one can think more clearly, and to think clearly is a necessary first step toward political regeneration." A good thought for personal reflection as we live in the midst of a perennial election season.

PROMOTING HUMAN WELFARE

Although it seems to get lost in the din of usual activities, August 19 is when we recognize World Humanitarian Day (the 19th). We have been noting and celebrating it since the United Nations established it in 2008. The impetus for the UN recognizing humanitarian activities was the 2003 bombing of the UN headquarters in Iraq. The day is set aside for compelling and important purposes, namely, "To recognize the compassion and bravery of humanitarian workers [and] to gain international cooperation to meet the needs of humanitarian work around the world."

A humanitarian is defined as "a person promoting human welfare and social reform." We are in the midst of an uncomfortable time involving transitions in attitudes and values about our past, our present, and our future. Historians will likely mark this time for generations yet to be born as a time of great and difficult change. The changes that are being called for are made more difficult by many who seem opposed to promoting human welfare and social reform. I think specifically of those who define cultural diversity as a threat, those who seem to endorse the cruelty of separating children from their parents and locking them in cages, those who think healthcare for all is not a human right, those who are not concerned about mounting poverty and economic injustices, and those unmoved by the centuries of racial oppression and abuse.

Thinking about what we are passing on to the next generations, I am somewhat buoyed by the words of Gandhi: "You must not lose faith in humanity. Humanity is an ocean; if a few drops of the ocean are dirty, the ocean does not become dirty." In my experience living and working on four continents, I agree that majorities of people do wish the best for others and do try to promote basic social fairness through reform. If only some of us would heed the words of Richard Nixon (yes, him!) when he said that Americans "cannot learn from one another until we stop shouting at one another." I was once advised that the more important the work, the smaller the voice to use. In other words, we are best served when we ignore the shouters, speak quietly, and get to work in caring about others.

As you experience the rest of this month of August, you may find that refreshing a spirit of humanitarianism in one's life can be renewing. How? Another dictionary defines a humanitarian as "a person who cares about people and who often participates in charity or does good work to show that care." Many, many acts fall into this category. Each of us can make a humanitarian effort by donating money to a larger organization that helps people, by reaching out to a person who is often left out at work or school, by donating to a local food pantry, by offering to babysit for free for a struggling family, or by taking many other such opportunities to make a difference that cross our lives daily. As Mother Teresa said, "If you can't feed a hundred people, feed just one."

GRAFTERS AND GRIFTERS

I'm still sometimes surprised at my limited vocabulary. Until the last few years, I had lived a fairly productive and mostly pleasant life without ever knowing anything about "wokeness." I confess that I have to say the same about the word *grifter*. I have now informed my understanding of wokeness, and hope you may appreciate my new learning about grifters. Having been born and raised in Iowa, I should have known about grifters. Its first use in the USA was in an Iowa newspaper, *The Waterloo Courier*. The 1902 article is about an unsavory businessman, a "grifter," being allowed to advertise his wares "by which he robs the merchants with his worthless trash."

Two years later, an article in the *St. Louis Republic* compared grifters and grafters, saying that "grafters, as everyone knows, are those who separate us from our earned or unearned increment in the ordinary course of business." The word *graft* first appeared in England in the late fifteenth century in the botanical sense. Once again, our American forebears gave it a darker meaning. Around 1865, according to the Oxford English Dictionary, the word *graft* in the US had become "the obtaining of profit or advantage by dishonest or shady means," especially "bribery, blackmail, or the abuse of a position of power or influence."

I was familiar with and have used the word *graft*. It was when many in the political world began accusing one another to be "grifters" that I took notice. One of the problems in finding the difference between *grifter* and *grafter* is that there appears to be some uncertainty of meaning in early use, especially with *grafter*. The *grifter* is typically defined as a small-time confidence man or some sort of a thief. The *grafter,* while also most of those things, may also be someone who engages in the "political corruption" sense of the word *graft*. Merriam-Webster defines such behavior as "the acquisition of money, position, or other profit by dishonest or questionable means, as by actual theft or by taking advantage of a public office or a position of trust or employment to obtain fees, perquisites, profits on contracts, or pay for work not done or service not performed."

So I've concluded that those who currently delight in calling a political adversary a "grifter" should really be using the word *grafter*! Why? Because they are describing someone who is engaged in the unfortunate old and current tradition of taking and using public money while not performing any public service while in office. As such, it is perhaps more accurate to choose *grafter* over *grifter*.

It makes me sad, and I am really tired of it. My mother and father, my kindergarten teacher, and many others always reminded me not to call people names. The Pulitzer Prize-winning American novelist, Toni Morrison, said this about such behavior: "Our debates, for the most part, are examples unworthy of a playground: name-calling, verbal slaps, gossip, giggles, all while the swings and slides of governance remain empty." I join those who also hope that the continuing election cycles may increasingly rid us of the name-callers and replace them with the hardworking do-gooders.

HOW LONG WILL IT TAKE?

I'm among the converted. I drive and love an electric car. We purchased our first electric vehicle twelve years ago. Over those years I've been asked many questions, heard many objections, suffered a few insults, and kept wondering why much of the public is so averse to transitioning to a technological and climatological improvement. So I ruminated and studied, and here is a very brief summary of what I found.

In the 1800s, the poor used the practical and sturdy ox, harnessed to a wagon, for longer trips. The well-to-do, who could afford a horse or several of them, used them for personal transportation. Most people, however, just walked, since almost all cities were no wider than two miles and easily walkable.

Beginning in America in the mid-nineteenth century, the Industrial Revolution found the horse to be one of the most remarkable primary movers on the planet. A horse could move people and goods wherever heavy steam locomotives could not and, especially, they could conquer terrible roads, which were a scourge of the nineteenth century. Yes, horses pretty much ruled nineteenth-century urban life and rural culture in both Europe and North America. And why not?

As Robert Thurston, who in 1894 was a US steam engine expert, pointed out, horses are not only "self-feeding, self-controlling, self-maintaining and self-reproducing, but they are far more economical in the energy they are able to develop from a given weight of fuel material, than any other existing form of motor."

Then, by the turn of the twentieth century, came the combustion engine and its application to vehicles. Interestingly, it took the automobile and tractor almost fifty years to displace the horse from farms, public transportation, and wagon delivery systems throughout America. But in opposition to what we often believe, the transition was neither smooth nor inevitable. And, as we are predicting will happen now as we transition from fossil fuels to electric, there were (and will be) winners and losers. Energy transitions can be messy.

Think of it this way: an energy system cannot be changed without hurting businesses, people, and the habits and practices that go with it. Most people who lose do so through no fault of their own, but simply because they are in a wrong place in history. Transitioning from horses to cars suffocated many businesses and professions, from carriage makers to teamsters. It drove down the price of grain so dramatically that the US Bureau of Census defined the horse-to-car transition as "one of the main contributing factors" to the Great Depression. And even though the automobile eliminated piles of manure and dead animals that clogged some nineteenth-century city streets, it also introduced a whole new set of global carbon complications, now threatening the very existence of our planet. So, cars didn't clean up our towns and cities but instead replaced stationary piles of dung with invisible clouds of pollution that moved with the wind and fed the growth of big government to help build roads to accommodate more cars.

In the end, removing horses from urban life and the farm became a fifty-year drama. It required the filthy adoption of three fossil-fuel technologies. It did not end the chaos in industrial cities but merely complicated and increased the movement of people and products. It did, however, illustrate two characteristics of energy transitions: they don't always solve problems, and they don't always perform as advertised. The difference now is that our planet's survival is at stake. Maybe we're lucky that one hundred years later, we Americans still hang onto our stubborn belief that there is a quick technological fix to every energy conundrum. I hope this time we'll be right.

ABOUT THE AUTHOR

Daniel C. Bruch, D.Min., Ph.D. Dr. Bruch is a retired professor and clergy. He has taught on the college, university, and seminary levels, including in Hungary, Romania, Serbia, and the Czech Republic. As a member of the clergy, he served two native churches at different times on the island of Bali in Indonesia, and as a university chaplain, a hospital emergency room chaplain, a police chaplain, a prison chaplain, and a parish pastor. He is a certified mediator and arbitrator, and a regular columnist at a regional newspaper. He currently serves as an online adjunct research professor at Framingham State University in Massachusetts. He has been married to Dr. Elizabeth Bruch for sixty-one years, and has four daughters, nine grandchildren, and two great-grandchildren.

www.ingramcontent.com/pod-product-compliance
Lightning Source LLC
Chambersburg PA
CBHW051110050726
47592CB00002B/759